Naim Attallah is chairman of the Namara Group and former chief executive of Asprey Plc.

By the same author

Women
Singular Encounters
Of a Certain Age
More of a Certain Age
Speaking for the Oldie
Asking Questions
A Timeless Passion
Tara & Claire

Forthcoming

In Conversation with Naim Attallah

A Woman a Week

BY
NAIM ATTALLAH

QUARTET BOOKS

First published by Quartet Books in 1998
A member of the Namara Group
27 Goodge Street
London W1P 2LD

Copyright © Naim Attallah 1998

All rights reserved. No part of this book may be reproduced in
any form or by any means without the prior written permission
of the publisher.

The moral right of the author has been asserted

A catalogue record for this book is available from the
British Library

ISBN 0 7043 8086 2

Phototypeset by The F.S.H. Group, London
Printed and bound in Great Britain by Cox & Wyman,
Reading, Berks

Preface

The idea for a column entitled *Woman of the Week* came from my friend Richard Addis, editor of *The Express*. He wanted a weekly feature on a woman of my choice.

The guiding principles have been topicality, notability and sometimes even notoriety. Political correctness has never been my strong point, and my section editor, Nigel Billen, has excelled himself in accommodating this failing.

Ten years ago I interviewed over three hundred women on fundamental issues ranging from sexuality and motherhood to feminism and creativity. This resulted in a mammoth volume entitled *Women*. I have never been the same since.

Having enjoyed the company of women all my life, I have always felt the need, almost a compulsion, to learn about them and to understand their dreams and aspirations. I am grateful to *The Express* for the opportunity to indulge this compulsion.

Naim Attallah, 1998

To women in their infinite variety

Joan Bakewell

Diane Blood

Clare Short

Fergie

In Praise of Ungentlemanly Conduct

Sir Compton Mackenzie, who was almost prosecuted for his novel, *Extraordinary Women*, once observed: 'Women do not find it difficult nowadays to behave like men, but they often find it extremely difficult to behave like gentlemen.'

This remark was not politically correct even 60 years ago when he made it, but it still has the ring of truth today. And thank goodness, because the ungentlemanly conduct of some women is riveting to the rest of us. Coupled with their ability to behave contrary to expectation, it is the stuff of journalists' dreams.

Ten years ago, I published a book entitled *Women*. My life was never the same again. I started off to interview 50 women, but ended up with nearly 300. Their beliefs were deeply personal, often startling, sometimes shocking. Ten years on, women have lost none of their edge. Just when you thought they might be content to sit back and take stock, they move into a different gear. Women – much more than men – constantly challenge stereotypes.

And so to this column. Each week it will be devoted to a woman in the news, someone who has perhaps tested our beliefs, altered public opinion or engaged our compassion. It will have the widest possible range and will not avoid sensitive issues. It will thrive on contradiction and controversy.

Last year was an excellent year for surprises. Who would have thought that Fergie would admit to insanity on the Ruby Wax Show? Or that Jerry Hall would take her knickers off for *Vogue*? Or that Jennifer Paterson and her fat friend would make obesity acceptable? Or that Joan Bakewell – once the Thinking Man's Crumpet, now champion of ethical issues – should turn out to have been Harold Pinter's mistress? It was also an interesting year for motherhood. We had a woman selectively aborting a healthy twin, then another who, by refusing that option, carried her eight unborn babies to certain death.

Then there was Clare Short, who was reunited with her adult son whom she gave up for adoption as a baby. Ten years ago, she told me that she had never had children because she was afraid of becoming her own mother. She went on to say: 'What is significant about being a parent is the loving and nurturing, helping a child to grow and being there all the time.' Was this the learning curve, or what?

It was even more astonishing that Diane Blood managed to milk the nation's sympathy with her campaign to be allowed to use her dead husband's sperm. Why did everyone see this endeavour as beautiful and good, rather than morbid and suspect? It gave me the creeps.

Perhaps the only woman who behaved entirely true to form was Gillian Shephard, who called for the return of caning. And why not? If it puts a stop to buggery, I'm all for it.

17TH JANUARY 1997

Princess Diana

Let the Princess fire with all cannons

On the face of it, Princess Diana and I have little in common. I am not as pretty as she is, I am still married, and my son is unlikely to be a future King of England. But there is one distinction which I share with the Princess: I, too, have been called a loose cannon. It was during my days as chief executive of a public company and my accuser was a city analyst who believed I had stepped out of line.

'Loose cannon' meant that I had ruffled a few feathers, that I had swum into the deep waters reserved for the big fish jealously guarding their territory and, above all, that I had upset the establishment. It seems that Princess Diana has done the same, and for that I applaud her.

In the old days, before the public scrubbing of dirty linen, much of the Princess's appeal lay in what appeared to be her innocence. If it was a myth, it was somehow a myth that one clung to out of a kind of benign optimism. The large, soulful eyes nourished one's faith. However, all illusions were shattered on *Panorama* when she emerged as bitter and manipulative. Her taste in men was also revealed as deplorable.

Of course, everyone is allowed one mistake. When she married Charles she was young and foolish and did not yet know the extent of the harm which had been done to him by the cold bath regime at Gordonstoun.

Failed marriages are one thing, but for Diana to have committed adultery with a saphead like Hewitt is beyond understanding. His single endowment seems to be located in what is referred to in Royal circles as the family jewels, but even that surely cannot compensate for overwhelming deficiencies in other departments.

With the royal divorce behind her, however, the Princess seems to have grown in stature. During the recent land-mine affair, the attempts by junior ministers to patronise her have made them look stupid and morally bankrupt. Their attitude is breathtaking in its arrogance. There is more mediocrity in politics than in any other profession. Most politicians are staggeringly self-regarding and talk more drivel than the so-called ordinary people whose intelligence they so often insult. To suggest that the Princess shouldn't meddle in something she doesn't understand is contemptuous: as if there were something deeply enigmatic about children whose limbs have been blown off, something that only Government ministers are capable of unravelling. You don't need to be aware of the intricacies of foreign policy to be appalled by mutilation and death, and to know that it is wrong. Princess Diana represents all of us who regard Government policy on land-mines as shaming and barbaric.

And so, loose cannons of the world unite. Let us continue to embarrass and rattle a few nerves. But a word of caution. Far be it from me to recommend the celibate life to a princess; but might I suggest that in future she chooses her men more carefully?

24TH JANUARY 1997

Lady Harlech

A DEDICATED FOLLOWER OF FASHION

The Brits have arrived. London is the hip city in Europe and positively shrieks with chic. It is now the inspiration of the fashion world, previously the reserve of the Europeans. First we exported stunning, aristocratic models to the catwalk, then our designers made a huge impact on *haute couture*. And now there is Lady Harlech, formerly Amanda Grieve, stoking the fires at the House of Chanel.

I knew her years ago when she was working at *Harpers & Queen* magazine and she was undoubtedly the most attractive girl about town. She lived her young life to the full, pushing back the boundaries until the boundaries caved in. Her talent and flair were not in doubt, but they were overshadowed by devilment.

When she was a student at Somerville College, Oxford, she broke hearts and captivated minds in equal measure. The extra dimension, the X factor which she possessed in exhilarating proportions, was a kind of elegant decadence which mesmerised all the young-blooded men of her generation and beyond.

Now married to an aristocrat and the mother of two children, she has become the hottest property in the fashion world. First she was the guiding light of Galliano, firing his imagination and influencing his collections with her own eccentric flourishes. Last month she succumbed to the lure of Lagerfeld, alias the Kaiser, now proudly showing his new acquisition to the world. Like a latter-day Henry V, his prayer has been answered: 'O for a Muse of fire, that would ascend/The brightest heaven of invention.'

Throughout history, English women abroad – often aristocratic, elegant and slightly dissolute – have worked a spell on powerful men. One thinks of Lady Hamilton, who inspired Nelson to victory over the French fleet and gave him the sort of welcome any man would love after his triumphal march through Naples. Or creative partnerships like that between the Italian film director Visconti and the deeply sensual Charlotte Rampling, whose erotic aura energised his talents. Already the fashion pundits are detecting Harlech's influence on Lagerfeld's new collection for Chanel. Style is hard to define, but easy to recognise: Harlech has style.

I have long supposed that there is a correlation between talent and decadence. Those women who lead an exemplary life are often dull and have little creativity. Those with a zest for life and a wayward disposition are often irresistibly attractive and successful.

In Dante's *Inferno*, Hell is described as a kind of conical funnel made up of successive circles to which the various categories of sinners are consigned. I would like to think that the terminally good are relegated to a special circle all of their own where they can bore each other to eternity. And I hope that God – with a twinkle in his eye – will favour the Amanda Harlechs of this world.

Surely, like Dante's Beatrice, they will inhabit *paradiso* on the top of the mountain, a realm of beauty and light and pleasure.

31ST JANUARY 1997

Camilla Parker Bowles

IT'S TIME TO END THE AGE OF CANT

Hypocrisy is alive and well and living in our midst. In the clamour of Tartuffes eager to pronounce on the relationship between Prince Charles and Camilla Parker Bowles, good sense has been lost in a smog of cant. Men of God and constitutional experts invoke the New Testament and the Establishment to help condemn two people to a lifetime of emotional poverty. A fitting punishment, some might say. After all it would never do to condone adultery.

History has been unkind to the adulterous woman. While men could be openly indifferent to their marriage vows, most fallen women ended up as social outcasts. Camilla Parker Bowles deserves a better fate. At the age of nearly 50, she has beaten all younger contenders to the heart of the Prince of Wales – a phenomenal achievement, given the array of pretty young things available.

The consensus view is that Camilla is not beautiful and that she lacks sex appeal. Yet those who sneer fail to grasp the significance of their own disdain; which is that Camilla has qualities which transcend the narrow range observable to the average individual.

She is undeniably intelligent and vivacious, and her friends speak of her great warmth and sincerity. Dignity has been the hallmark of her behaviour. While everyone else has been queuing up to sell their stories, she has maintained a regal silence. This is evidence of a love far deeper than its distant cousins, Caprice and Frivolity. It is not a fairy-tale love, which the British seem to crave. Camilla's devotion to Charles has a much sounder base. And the Camillagate tapes show that their private conversations have an element of crudeness – a welcome sign of normality. Even Jane Austen was occasionally coarse in letters to her sister.

In David Lean's film, *Brief Encounter*, Trevor Howard and Celia Johnson are the doomed couple who put their own marriages before love and happiness. Great British values are upheld at the expense of pain and suffering. While the film was a huge post-war success, it is now evocative of a lost age.

We may not approve of divorce, but it is a fact of modern times. There is little point in Charles and Camilla choosing a life of misery and denial to pander to our refined sensibilities. Unlike the protagonists in *Brief Encounter*, they are both free to marry. There is no impediment, save the excessive piety and meddling of the nation. Nothing they have done has exceeded the normal patterns of human frailty and sinfulness.

Given a chance, Camilla could be the very making of Charles. She could temper his eccentricity (unbecoming in a young man), restore his dignity (lost during his whinging to Jonathan Dimbleby) and transform him into a stable, happy man. She would erase the memory of freezing baths at Gordonstoun by bringing passion and comfort to his bed. In the process, she would become an icon of womanhood, an exultation of maturity over youth; above all both feminism and femininity would triumph.

7TH FEBRUARY 1997

Patsy Kensit

SUCH GOLDEN PROMISE TURNED TO DUST

The idea of lost innocence is as old as creation. Since the beginning of time we have been trying to understand the wickedness of the world and those who fall by the wayside. The latest chapter in the life of Patsy Kensit together with the media hype illustrate a double decline: the dissoluteness of the happy couple themselves matched only by the mad antics of those who pursue them.

For days on end the newspapers have been full of excited speculation, as if serial marriages were football matches rather than the stuff of tragedy. Such behaviour demeans us all. If there is a real story to be told it contains more pity and sadness than the headlines would suggest.

I interviewed Patsy Kensit when she was just 17 years old. This was soon after she starred in *Absolute Beginners*. The film was not a critical success but it made her name, and from that moment onwards the cameras followed her wherever she went. We talked at length and we kept in touch for a time. She had all the verve of youth and an unworldliness which was very engaging. Her stunning looks coupled with a kind of childlike grace made her irresistibly attractive and strangely vulnerable. These were the same qualities which she brought to the BBC's *Silas Marner* when she played the faithful Eppie, more precious to Silas than his lost fortune in gold.

That such golden promise should have turned to dust contains a certain poignancy. Yet Patsy Kensit would seem to have been the architect of her own destiny. In recent years she has embarked on a downward spiral of behaviour and in the process she has lost her most endearing qualities. She has become addicted to the feckless glamour and sleaze of the rock scene with all its ugly trappings. The intemperate language and spoilt-child tantrums are not in the least becoming. But of course bad manners and coarse behaviour are contagious, and Liam Gallagher is not exactly the boy next door.

At 28 Patsy Kensit has two failed marriages behind her and a four-year-old child, an innocent victim in the drama. It is a strange irony that when she herself was aged four she made her film debut in *The Great Gatsby* as Mia Farrow's daughter, also a casualty of the fast lane.

Does life imitate art? It is well known that early experiences imprint on the minds of young children and their impact becomes clear only much later.

The Great Gatsby is based on Scott Fitzgerald's novel about the shallowness of the American dream. It is a world of terrifying moral emptiness inhabited by people who have too much money and precious few manners. Glamour and squalor are held in grim equilibrium.

In the end Fitzgerald's story transcends its own bitter view. We must trust that Patsy Kensit can find the inner resources to do the same; otherwise her future looks bleak. I once sent her a silver heart. I hope it will bring her luck.

14TH FEBRUARY 1997

Elizabeth Hurley

Paying the High Price of Fame

*I*n Gilbert & Sullivan's *The Mikado* there is a farcical scene in which Katisha proclaims: 'I have a left shoulder-blade that is a miracle of loveliness. People come miles to see it. My right elbow has a fascination that few can resist!' Somehow this sprang to mind when Liz Hurley appeared this week in her designer undies at the celebrations for Elizabeth Taylor's 65th birthday.

The similarity between Hurley and Katisha is in their desperation to be taken seriously – at once sad and comic – and the self-defeating manner in which this is effected.

The most important single factor which propelled Liz Hurley into the world of fashion and beauty was That Dress, the one held together by safety pins. Her subsequent disclaimer that the outfit was lent to her by Versace at the last minute and that she tried it on in the lavatory has a certain fanciful ring. The truth is, she loves the limelight and is a dab hand at trying to capture it, even when the occasion is in honour of a woman of substance.

There is nothing actually wrong with this. Appearing half-naked in public is something Miss Hurley does extremely well. I am as delighted as the next man to feast on her physical endowments, although there is little challenge to the imagination. The old black and white films were far more erotic than their modern equivalents because they were understated.

Miss Hurley is undergoing something of a crisis. Her first film production, *Extreme Measures*, has been blasted by the critics in America as mediocre and lacking plausibility. She longs for intellectual credibility and critical endorsement, but they continue to elude her. This is because her image is entirely at variance with her aspiration. Those who proclaim Grant and Hurley the new Burton and Taylor have been duped by their own hype. Hurley has the looks of Taylor, but not the magic. Taylor's vital spirit is informed by intelligence and a kind of emotional honesty. She could fight like a tigress, but her integrity was never in doubt. 'I want to be known as an actress. I am not royalty,' she once said. By contrast, Hurley is far less than the sum of her (quite beautiful) parts. She is also controlled to the point of being glacial.

She could have taken a different route. Ten years ago she showed real potential in the title role of Dennis Potter's *Christabel* for the BBC. Dennis, who considered it a fine piece of acting, must now be spinning in his grave.

The novelist Muriel Spark once said that writers sin against God because they create characters who cannot bring about their own salvation. Miss Hurley is not yet the stuff of fiction; there is still time for her to save herself. But while she is The Face at Estée Lauder and The Body at every film première, she has to be realistic about her more earnest ambitions. In the meantime, she must be content to be famous for being famous.

21st February 1997

Koo Stark

Adding a touch of Stark reality

From soft porn to full-term pregnancy is a spectacular coming of age. At the beginning of the century, unmarried mothers were stigmatised as immoral and forced into the workhouse; now Koo Stark has helped turn the single mother into a sex symbol, the very epitome of *fin-de-siècle* morality.

Koo has always been unpredictable, and her journey, undertaken in the spotlight of the cameras, has included a number of interesting milestones. It all began with her erotic rites-of-passage movie, *Emily*, which I saw soon after meeting her for the first time. The film is provocative and contains moments of carnality which are guaranteed to make strong men quiver.

Some years later, she varied the theme by breathing fire and passion into the royal family through her 18-month association with Prince Andrew. In so doing, she became both a media target and darling of the rich and famous. She played her role supremely well, never putting a foot wrong, never committing the slightest indiscretion.

Many believe she would have made an excellent wife for the prince. Whereas Fergie is vulgar, Koo is distinguished. In place of tackiness, she would have injected glamour and a certain intelligence. She would also have helped the monarchy survive the millennium by introducing the common touch – rather than the common behaviour which has infected them like a chronic illness.

Koo Stark is a complex character. She longs to be taken seriously, perhaps to dispel the *femme fatale* image. She need not worry; it is by no means unusual for actresses to engage in risqué films to give impetus to their ambitions. Indeed, it is to their credit if they go on to reinvent themselves, as Koo has done most successfully as a photographer much admired by the late Norman Parkinson.

She has always blossomed in the public gaze. We once attended a Broadway première together where the screaming paparazzi knocked us to the ground. It was a frightening experience, but Koo is a professional and took it in her stride. She has the ability to embrace each new situation with confidence.

Pregnancy in itself is not a phenomenon, even though at 40 the stakes are higher. What has made Koo Stark's incipient motherhood the focus of attention is her refusal to disclose the identity of the father – not, in fact, an unprecedented manoeuvre. There is, of course, a certain irony in making publicity out of a secret. The irony becomes all the more bizarre when we consider that she chose to announce her reticence on the subject in *Hello* magazine, the last refuge of the down-and-outs of café society. 'I certainly believe my child has a right to know his [father's] name first.'

Quite so. Having consulted my handbook on child development, I gather that, unless Koo's child is unusually precocious, we cannot expect him to utter the immortal words: 'Who is my daddy?' much before the age of five. Until then we must hold our breath in agonised anticipation.

28TH FEBRUARY 1997

The Spice Girls

Homage to Thatcher's Children

Mrs Thatcher once said: 'Everyone should have a Willy.' Although the context was a discussion about William Whitelaw, the remark seemed to have a significance greater than her immediate reference. Fifteen years on, the outrageous Spice Girls are proving themselves to be true Thatcher's children. Consider the recent boast of Geri: 'We've all got balls, but I've got quite big balls, basically.' This is real girl power.

Geri also suggested that Mrs T was the original Spice Girl. The Iron Lady may have been old-fashioned, but she handbagged ruthlessly. She was spirited and spunky, fiercely patriotic and she recognised the value of high achievement and the struggle involved. 'Life's a continuous business,' she intoned, 'requiring continuous effort.' This is the obvious antecedent of Mel B's tongue-studded pronouncement: 'Life in general is f***ing hard.'

This year's Brit Awards confirmed that the Spice Girls are now the biggest band on the music scene. They have entered our language as a metaphor for irrepressible ebullience, unpredictability and a complete lack of inhibition. In true Thatcherite style they are batting for Britain, making huge amounts of money for the country and boosting the economy. They all have distinctive attributes, but there is a synergy which exceeds the sum of their individual impact. Taken together, they are like volatile substances in a chemistry set.

Those who are scandalised by their language and brash behaviour have missed the point. Each decade has its own trajectory. The Sixties were notorious for the shift from innocence to experience, from hope to rage, from idealism to nihilism. Now the concepts are less well-defined and it is easy to feel threatened by a bunch of girls fooling around in the murky waters somewhere between intemperance and an enviable lack of constraint.

In fact, their rough brand of humour is so extreme as to be innocuous. Those who speak of unacceptable boundaries being crossed ought to enter the real world. They remind me of Mary Whitehouse and her Festival Of Light trying to whip up public indignation over Monty Python's *Life of Brian*, branding the film sick when it was merely screwball entertainment.

The Spice Girls are a breath of fresh air in a country polluted by conventions and restrictions. We need a cultural revolution to rid us of the tired values of the establishment – hypocrisy, reserve, secrecy. If only our present cabinet ministers would gyrate more and pontificate less, if only they would inject the same passion into their policies as the Spice Girls do into their song-and-dance act, then the whole political spectrum might be transformed. In the meantime – as Posh Spice bluntly suggests – we are governed by boring pillocks.

7TH MARCH 1997

Sophie Dahl

Yes, Big Really Can Be Beautiful

Size isn't everything. Genitally-challenged men have traditionally found solace in these words, but when it comes to women and fashion, there is no comfort to be had. Models dictate the ideal to which other women must aspire and it has long been a sad fact that size *is* everything. Ever since Twiggy in the Sixties, there has been a succession of emaciated little girls from the fashion houses. It was therefore particularly pleasing during London Fashion Week to see Sophie Dahl, six feet tall and size 14, step confidently onto the catwalk.

Miss Dahl, granddaughter of the writer Roald Dahl, understandably caused quite a stir. She displayed a femininity and a fullness of flesh more in keeping with a Rubens painting than the half-starved creatures so favoured by our multi-million pound designer industry.

The perception of what women should look like has long been dictated by men, a tyranny in which – whatever the feminists may say – women have colluded. Our cultural fixation on female thinness has more to do with control than beauty. Curves are actually beautiful and sensual, and fat is a symbol of fertility – something which was appreciated in every century until our own. Representations of the female nude traditionally gloried in the natural shape of women.

Nowadays, the vogue is haggard and unhealthy, the androgynous look often reflecting the sexual ambiguity of male designers. It is an absurdity of tragic proportions that many models are so thin that their natural cycles are damaged and their fertility diminished. We must hope that Sophie Dahl can reverse a dangerous trend and undo some of the harm wrought on generations of young girls.

I have a soft spot for the Dahl family. I know Tessa Dahl, Sophie's mother, from my days in film production, and her father, Roald, was a man of exceptional talent and imagination. About 15 years ago, he wrote a controversial piece in the *Literary Review* of which I am proprietor. With characteristic wryness, he apparently told his daughter that I had stopped him receiving a knighthood.

Roald Dahl would surely have been proud of his granddaughter. In many of his stories he has a penchant for substantial women on whom he endows larger than life qualities in keeping with their size. His bizarre story *Georgy Porgy*, typical of the genre, portrays a tiny repressed clergyman and one of his female parishioners – a striking person, unusually muscular for a woman, with broad shoulders and powerful arms and a huge calf bulging on each leg. The wimpish man is so intimidated by this large woman that he comes to believe that she has literally swallowed him – an insane conviction which Dahl brings off with a touch of genius.

Like Dahl's heroine, Sophie appears to be a woman of strong appetites. Indeed, she looks as if she might devour a few of the stick insect types for breakfast. However, if she can help restore women's confidence in their natural shape, she will be true to the spirit she carries in her genes.

14TH MARCH 1997

Isabelle Ayasch
Edith Cresson

A SEVERE CASE OF CHUNNEL VISION

Chesterton once said: 'If an Englishman has understood a Frenchman, he has understood the most foreign of foreigners.' Ever since the Norman Conquest in 1066, mutual mistrust and suspicion have reigned between France and Britain. Napoleon called the British a nation of shopkeepers, while George Bernard Shaw considered the French to be born pedants. The average Frenchman believes that the British lack style and culture, that their food is inedible and that they are sexually retarded. The British counterblast is to regard the French as a bunch of peasants with unpleasant body odours and awful lavatories and speaking a language which consists of making funny noises through the nose which normal people cannot possibly emulate.

Isabelle Ayasch, author of a recent textbook to be used in French schools, is merely the latest to endorse the Anglo-French trade in insults. She displays a richly jaundiced view of Britain, claiming that 'the British have a superiority complex that makes it hard for them to accept the Empire no longer exists'. She suggests that the young people of this country are 'intellectually and morally poor and lack principles' and that 'single mothers are unacquainted with the notions of ambition, duty, punctuality and the improvement of the self'. Predictably, this onslaught has provoked a counter-attack of similar proportions in British newspapers – which, incidentally, Isabelle Ayasch considers to be 'vulgar, insolent and a tool of the establishment'.

This most recent episode in the *entente cordiale* is reminiscent of a skirmish six years ago in which I had a personal involvement. In 1991, a Sunday newspaper ran my interview with France's first woman Prime Minister, Edith Cresson, in which she was remarkably forthcoming on the subject of sex, in particular the failings of the English male of the species whom she considered weak, cold-blooded and superficial. 'Frenchmen are much more interested in women; Anglo-Saxon men are not. I don't know whether it is cultural or biological, but there is something there that isn't working – that's obvious.' However, her most extravagant claim was that 25 per cent of Englishmen were homosexual – a comment which almost caused a diplomatic incident. A Conservative MP raised the matter in the House of Commons, inviting the Speaker to agree that Madame Cresson had insulted the virility of the British male. Mr Speaker, wearing stockings and a curly wig at the time, replied: 'The virility of members is not a matter for me.'

The difference between Ayasch and Cresson is not one of conviction but of perspective. Cresson based her views on personal experience whereas Ayasch claims scholarship. Defending her book as 'totally unbiased', she cites her credentials (university lecturer who studied at Oxford) – before saying: 'The time has come for the British to accept that they are not God's gift to the universe.' Those familiar with the works of Descartes, Pascal, Rousseau and Montaigne will not, perhaps, detect an obvious luminary in the great French academic league. But in keeping with tradition she has stoked the fires of discord.

21ST MARCH 1997

Lady Thatcher

Cause of a Major disagreement

Lady Thatcher's most recent endorsement of John Major is probably the sweet kiss of death. Was there ever a more disingenuous blessing from woman to man? She announced her support for him in front of the cameras as if she were reporting a blocked drain to visiting sanitary inspectors. The mystery – if there is one – lies in the masquerade, since she has lost no opportunity to undermine Mr Major while fluttering her eyelids at Mr Blair.

On a number of occasions during her term of office I requested an interview with Lady Thatcher. She always declined, politely but firmly, and I think I know why. Two years after she had been elected leader of the Conservative party, my publishing house Quartet Books brought out a package called *Mrs Thatcher's Bag*.

The stylish blue handbag contained a mask, a cut-out doll and clothes by John Kent, a record called *Maggie's Song* featuring George Melly, a campaign button to confound the Socialists and a tasteful poster containing the leader's Pearls of Wisdom. There was also a pamphlet by John Wells entitled: *Managing – A Guide To Modern Etiquette By Margaret Hilda Thatcher*. It was dedicated to the memory of the Rt Hon Lady Macbeth, Countess of Glamis, A Great Tory Who Knew What She Wanted. All good clean fun and perfectly harmless but, according to Press reports, Mrs Thatcher was furious. Unlike Denis, she appears to lack a sense of humour.

When people are suffering from dementia, some enlightened doctors apparently ask certain questions to assess the severity of impairment. These are generally simple tests of memory to do with dates or family history. When it comes to the question: 'Who is our Prime Minister?' those poor souls who cannot even remember their own birthdays still answer with alacrity: 'Mrs Thatcher'. Seven years after she left office this is a remarkable phenomenon. Whatever our views, her place in history is assured.

Some years ago, I appeared on Jonathan Dimbleby's *Any Questions*. The last question to the panel invited the men to imagine which woman they would most like to be. At first my mind was a complete blank. But in an instant, as with those on the brink of senility, a figure with hooded eyes and a handbag filled the empty space. 'I would like to be Mrs Thatcher!' I declared. The reaction of the audience was hostile, and so I tried to dig myself out of a hole by praising her energy and determination.

The following week I sat next to Germaine Greer at a lunch. She too attacked me for choosing Mrs Thatcher and produced a left hook by asking me: 'Have you considered that if you were Mrs Thatcher you would have to sleep with Denis?' This blow to the head concentrated the faculties beautifully and my mind felt clearer than ever before. Next time I think I will be Pamela Anderson.

28TH MARCH 1997

Jenny Agutter

Timeless charm despite Hollywood hassle

Favourite old films, like much-loved childhood haunts, can be dangerous territory to revisit after the passage of many years. Finding a beloved place altered and therefore violated has its painful counterpart in the cinema when we discover the old magic has gone from the modern revival. Yet there is no disenchantment with *The Railway Children*, re-released last week after nearly 30 years.

The story of an Edwardian family in crisis retains its timeless charm, thanks to Jenny Agutter's memorable performance as the sensible older sister. The button boots and starched petticoats, the steam trains and stoicism, the sweep of the Yorkshire Dales and the fierce family loyalties – they are solid mooring points in a world all but vanished. The enduring image of Jenny Agutter standing bravely on the railway track, flagging down the London train with her red-flannel underclothes is vintage cinema.

It is also an image which most would have found difficult to live down. A child actor with great talent is a joy to behold, but the transition to the harsh Hollywood climate is often a difficult one. Jenny Agutter has never achieved the level of stardom accorded to actresses like Emma Thompson or Kate Winslet. This is probably due to her modesty and unworldliness which have always distinguished her both on and off stage. She glows in a cloudless sky; she does not cause electric storms. Her sex appeal is benign, and although she has taken her clothes off in several films, the nudity has always seemed artistic and integral to the film, rather than a Glenda Jackson-type romp.

When she swam naked in Nicolas Roeg's *Walkabout*, it was a hauntingly beautiful scene. She plays a girl lost in the outback with her younger brother, and although the Australian film eschews the sentimentality of *The Railway Children*, there are similarities between the two. They both deal with rites of passage and there is a wistfulness for a time when things were happier and more certain. Most importantly, perhaps, the simplicity of both stories is deceptive; it belies the larger, metaphorical overtones of the child's innocence which is not only lost, but cannot ever be recovered.

When I interviewed her 10 years ago, Jenny Agutter still seemed a slightly ethereal young girl with old-fashioned values. She told me how uncomfortable she felt with the pressures of Hollywood, the need to sell herself, the requirement to be seen at the right parties. She spoke with candour and self-effacement about the difficulties of being expected to be someone she was not. She confessed to feeling 'alien', in the sense of being different from those whose experience she apparently shared. 'You have to recognise the division between the way you feel emotionally and logically . . . I have not been able to settle down.'

With marriage and motherhood, Jenny Agutter appears finally to have settled down. The fulfilment she has found is in keeping with the happy ending of a magical old film.

4 FEBRUARY 1997

Anita Roddick

Peppermint Oil on Troubled Consciences

*I*t is rumoured that the saintly Anita Roddick was once in heaven before she came to inhabit our terrestrial planet. In her celestial existence, she demonstrated the same ingenuity and marketing skills which she was to use so effectively in her subsequent role as Evangelist of the Earth.

The Spirit Shop, a divine chain of outlets containing products to nourish the soul, was not, alas, a runaway success. True, there was a steady demand for her jojoba and coconut oil to anoint the holy fathers at special ceremonies. And the angels, who have the freedom to exercise moral choices, were much taken with Galilean Gel, perfect for putting a shine on their wings. But, even in heaven, Anita's excessive preaching tried the patience of Job.

Her Cleanliness Next To Godliness range made repentant sinners long nostalgically for sackcloth and ashes. The crunch came as she proclaimed the noble properties of her Peppermint With Piety Lotion; her halo, made by Cayapo Indian converts to Christianity, grated discordantly against the glass ceiling of the firmament. Miss Roddick was too good for Heaven. She had to go.

Relocation on earth provided the challenge she needed. Millions of people were persuaded to pamper their bodies while gently massaging their moral sense. Moreover – and herein lies the real genius – they could be kind to themselves without pillaging the planet –

something only nasty cosmetics companies did. Thus, the Body Shop was born and sprang up all over the world like organically-grown mushrooms.

Morality became a new and wonderful consumer product. Exhortations to good behaviour ('Do you really *need* a carrier bag?') were excellent for business and gave the customer a warm glow at no extra charge. Exfoliate your face and wipe away the sins of the world. Ice-Blue Shampoo is good for you and saves the whale, too.

Meanwhile, Miss Roddick waged war on her competitors: 'Their major product lines are packaging and garbage.' Much better to have little bottles of carrot shampoo nestling on a basket of shredded paper swathed in plastic with a dinky stick-on bow.

Soon, Anita became a scintilla of light struggling against the forces of darkness. The purity of her products was matched only by the purity of her motives. Principles were the thing, not profits. Some analysts suggested her green image was a touch too verdant and that her Trade Not Aid policy made exaggerated claims, but beautiful pictures of Anita with Amazonian Indians beamed down from Body Shop walls. This is big business with a heart. We know that from the television commercial in which Anita is seen bonding with Mexican villagers while singing the praises of American Express.

Her recent attack on women's magazines coincides with the announcement of her own proposed publication, *Full Voice*. It is aimed at 'real women' who refuse to be manipulated by the industry. Virtue is its own reward, but the case for canonisation is now conclusive.

11TH APRIL 1997

Elizabeth Taylor

A STAR TAYLOR-MADE FOR HOLLYWOOD

According to Greek legend, the phoenix is a rare bird which, after a long and interesting life, builds itself a funeral pyre, flaps its wings to fan the flames, and burns itself to death; whereupon it rises from the ashes with renewed life to start the cycle all over again. The human equivalent of this fabulous bird is Elizabeth Taylor – a legend in her own lifetime. She has flirted with death a number of times, but just when people have imagined the light was finally to be extinguished, she has risen like Lazarus from her sick bed.

Elizabeth Taylor personifies the difficulties of Hollywood fame. Child stars were huge box office draws in the early Forties, and Taylor's exceptional beauty, together with the radiant charm she brought to films such as *National Velvet*, provided symbols of optimism during the war years.

The height of her career was between the mid-Fifties and Sixties when her acting roles mirrored the intensity and passion of her own life. She was nominated for an Oscar for her portrayal of mental breakdown in *Raintree County*, and in her Academy Award winning *Who's Afraid of Virginia Woolf?* she ranted and raved to maintain the illusion of control in a dismal life laid waste by heavy drinking.

Off-stage she reveals extraordinary self-knowledge and a disarming candour. Perhaps because of her own awareness of the frailty of life, she has extended great charity towards others. She started the American Foundation for AIDS research which has raised millions of dollars. She is revered in America – more celebrated than the First Lady.

Her succession of marriages has been a remarkable triumph of eternal hope over personal experience. She has always married for love, and divorced in sorrow. To walk down the aisle twice with the same man (Richard Burton) requires courage and imagination. For Mike Todd, son of a rabbi, she even converted to Judaism. This led to her remark on taking the title role in *Cleopatra*: 'It will be fun to be the first Jewish Queen of Egypt.' Even when she was in rehabilitation for drug and alcohol abuse, she still managed to fall in love. Before her wedding to Larry Fortensky, her eighth husband 20 years her junior, she announced to the world: 'We want to spend the rest of our lives together.' That this marriage was also dissolved indicates folly perhaps, but not cynicism.

In addition to husbands she has had some strange relationships. Of her close friend Michael Jackson, she once said: 'He is the least weird man I have ever met.' If this remark was made in good faith, it reveals less about Jackson and more about the idiosyncratic nature of Taylor.

The recent extravaganza for her 65th birthday followed by her operation for a brain tumour provided us with live theatre.

Elizabeth Taylor has given focus to the fantasies of several generations. Her life is drawn in epic dimensions, but her story is principally a saga of survival.

18 APRIL 1997

Christine Hamilton

Exploding the Myth of the Gentler Sex

*T*hose who witnessed Christine Hamilton's ambush of the hapless Martin Bell may have wondered how on earth we managed to lose the Empire. A visiting Martian, on the basis of his observation of the Tatton Siege, would certainly have found it difficult to believe that women were once oppressed. As the shrill voice boomed out again and again: 'Do you accept my husband is innocent?', it was just possible for a moment to feel sorry for Neil Hamilton.

Depending on political affiliations and other prejudices, Mrs Hamilton may variously be seen as an asset, a liability, or a weapon in the armoury of Tory Tatton. If a weapon, then definitely high explosive and deadly: exocet missile, rather than pea-shooter.

Political wives come in a variety of shapes and forms. There is the now familiar stand-by-your-man Tory type who fights back the tears and stays loyally by her husband's side for the sake of the cameras and the marriage. Then there is the Norma Major model who is uncomfortable in the limelight but does what is required of her with a good grace. Others, like the Chancellor's wife, seem to have taken a vow of silence and appear only when absolutely required by the occasion.

Christine Hamilton is none of these. Not for her the anonymity of the wings; she much prefers centre stage, leading from the front, shooting from the hip. Cast firmly in the Lady Macbeth mould, her absoluteness of purpose, her ambition, her control of the situation would not have been out of place in Inverness Castle. This is no fanciful comparison. During the Hamiltons' appearances in the constituency – always as a double-act with Mrs Hamilton looking to be firmly in command – the MP has seemed weak and emasculated by her side. Her disconcerting habit of leading him around by the hand has overtones of Lady Macbeth steering her husband away from the scene of the crime.

As her husband's secretary, she has devoted herself to his career. She is at the very epicentre of what has been called the 'web of influence' which is causing the present outcry over sleaze. But like many who do not suffer from self-doubt, she has a disarming way of claiming the moral high ground while blaming all those who do not share the 'correct' view. The moral indignation is palpable.

In our culture there is a persistent fable: women, being gentler than men, the sharers and carers of our species, are consequently more moral; given the chance they would purify the government of corruption, put an end to war and make the world a safer place.

I love and admire women, invariably giving them the benefit of the doubt. But Mrs Hamilton is unbearably testing, and everything about her explodes the myth of the gentler sex.

25 APRIL 1997

Stella McCartney

WILL YOU STILL LOVE ME WHEN I AM FAMOUS TOO?

'They f*** you up, your mum and dad./They may not mean to, but they do.' In these two short lines, the poet Philip Larkin articulated a great truth. Despite their best intentions, sometimes because of them, parents can scarcely avoid visiting huge burdens upon their children. If they are also rich and famous, the burdens are invariably heavier.

The news that Stella McCartney has been appointed chief designer at the House of Chloe in Paris was greeted by the rasping sound of knives being sharpened. As the daughter of two famous parents, and as a relative *ingénue* in the world of fashion, her success is inevitably attributed to her name rather than native talent. Karl Lagerfeld, whose job Stella has taken over, did not even try to disguise his disdain, and Luisa Beccaria, passed over for the post, was openly contemptuous: 'Who is she? What has she done?' Nearer home, another commentator sneered: 'It's just a big PR stunt.'

The catwalk is aptly named. The unpleasant yowling and screeching accompanying this appointment would rival any bunch of mangy alley cats. There is no reason why we should be surprised, given the British dislike of success and our culture of envy. People will scorn and cry, 'Foul!' even when the evidence offers little support.

Paul and Linda McCartney strove to give their

children as normal an upbringing as possible. Like her siblings, Stella attended a junior state school in northwest London before going to a local comprehensive when the family moved to East Sussex. She then studied at St Martin's School of Art and Design, but she also took time out to learn the skills of traditional tailoring with Edward Sexton in Knightsbridge. Of course, it may be that she has used her famous parentage to gain an entrée into the exclusive world of *haute couture* – it would be extraordinary if her name did not work to her advantage. But now, she will have to prove herself worthy of the post beyond any measure of hereditary privilege. The pressure on her to succeed is immense.

Talent – whoever possesses it – always needs nurturing. About 20 years ago, I backed an aspiring young woman who wanted to break into the fashion world. She had enthusiasm and determination, but lacked experience and material support. Her name was Arabella Pollen and she went on to design for café society girls, including the youthful Princess Diana.

The cynical among us would do well to remember that fame and privilege can be a curse as well as a blessing. Think of Randolph Churchill who died a sad and bitter man, or his sister Diana, who committed suicide. Mary Soames, youngest of the Churchills, wrote that her parents grieved over the shipwrecks of their children. Think of Marlon Brando's son, or the Marquesses of Blandford and Bristol. Given the extreme perils, Stella McCartney has so far acquitted herself well. She could easily be lying stoned among the dossers in the Strand.

2ND MAY 1997

Selina Scott

Great Scott, Selina's Trumped Again

Other people's feuds are usually entertaining, often embarrassing, sometimes shameful. If they serve any useful purpose, it is to dissuade the rest of us from the indignity of similar entanglements. Once again, it is open warfare between multi-millionaire Donald Trump and television presenter Selina Scott. The row broke out two years ago after Trump was interviewed by Scott for a TV documentary. Her portrait of the fast-talking Yankee tycoon was violently at odds with his own self-image.

Hell hath no fury like a male ego dented and there followed a barrage of invective from across the Atlantic. Ironically, the nature of the insults shed more light on Trump's character than the most penetrating interview could have done. The manner of his attack was particularly instructive. In a letter to Scott, he first of all established his own pre-eminence: 'Up until last spring, I had never heard of you.' (Subtext: The fact that I had never heard of you is clear evidence of your inferior status.)

Now that Selina Scott's ratings on the Sky 1 talk show have plummeted to insupportable levels, Trump is once again firing off poison darts. They appear to have hit their target, since Selina is claiming that his behaviour towards her is a form of mental stalking.

Like all the most engaging women, Selina Scott is complex and sexually mysterious. I first met her more than 10 years ago and greatly enjoyed her company. We fell out when she withdrew from an interview for my book *Women*, and a chill wind blew for some years till we met again at a BAFTA dinner, where we kissed and made up. When she made her début on *News At Ten*, she caused strong men to drool and go weak at the knees. After newscasting, she quickly rose to celebrity status as interviewer of the rich and famous.

Part of the enigma is that she has lived through a number of gaffes and self-inflicted wounds, most notably during the Booker Prize presentation when she failed to recognise one of the judges and asked her if she had read all the novels on the shortlist.

Perhaps the old Bob Dylan song, *Love Minus Zero*, got it right – there's no success like failure, but inevitably her survival has led to spiteful suggestions that beauty has held sway over brains. In fact, Selina has never scaled the intellectual heights, but her other qualities are greatly to be valued among the hard and clinical attitudes which prevail in television journalism. There is no denying her attractiveness, but that is hardly a crime.

Selina is at her best when she eschews affectation and stops fluttering her eyelashes. She is warm and flirtatious which is a lot better than being frigid and aggressive. Life can be tough at the top and no doubt many will rejoice in her latest difficulties. But she is a survivor. The chances are the gods will continue to smile upon her.

9TH MAY 1997

Ann Widdecombe

The Tories' prophetess of doom

Ann Widdecombe's assertion that Michael Howard's personality contains 'something of the night' charts new waters in the high seas of political disparagement. Its strength lies in its sinister insinuation, the hint of menace and foreboding, the biblical *gravitas* ('And God called the light Day and the darkness he called Night'). It also concurs with our own worst fears about the former Home Secretary. Who among us has not been troubled by the demonic gleam in his eye, the smirk on his smug face?

This modern clash of the Titans makes for dream journalism. It has all the necessary ingredients for good copy – man and woman locked in battle, allegations of impropriety, romantic innuendo (flowers and chocolates). Both contestants are without fear and – in their own way – quite terrifying.

Miss Widdecombe is a particularly intrepid opponent. She once took on the Archbishop of Canterbury, accusing him of presiding over chaos in the Church of England, her spiritual home. In an open letter to Dr Carey, she wrote of 'heads buried in the sands of eternal compromise' and claimed the Church was 'run by lemmings'.

Miss Widdecombe is neither ostrich nor lemming. In 1992, she left the Church of England after the General Synod voted in favour of women priests. The following year, she converted to Roman Catholicism and pronounced: 'To have a church which calls a sin a sin is a blessed relief.' She speaks in absolutes, her language seeming to belong to a vanished age. The academic rigour and the moral rigidity perfectly reflect her classical education and religious faith.

I am always slightly ill at ease with people who are so certain of everything. I am a Roman Catholic myself, but it is not clear to me how someone can both be fanatically pro-life when it comes to a sensitive issue like abortion, and fervently pro-death when it comes to capital punishment. The Pope may be infallible, but the English judiciary is not.

Miss Widdecombe performs a difficult balancing act between promoting the individual freedom staunchly advocated by her party, while accepting unequivocally the authority of the Church. It is something she does well against formidable odds. Because of her shape and unmarried status, she has been the victim of savage insolence and cruelty, both borne with fortitude.

At her confirmation, Miss Widdecombe took the name of Hugh after the 16th-century martyr Bishop Hugh Latimer whose last words as he burnt in the flames were: 'We shall this day light such a candle by God's grace in England as shall never be put out.'

I am not sure that the state of beatitude awaits Ann Widdecombe. Although her views are sincerely held, she is too brisk, too crisp, too full of rebuke. But she has undoubtedly lit a candle to Mr Howard's character. She utters the words 'something of the night' with the authority of Cassandra, prophetess of doom. Those of us familiar with classical mythology will remember that Cassandra's predictions were invariably correct.

16TH MAY 1997

Janet Street-Porter

Yoof Culture's Strange Phenomenon

Man is a naturally curious animal, but every so often one craves ignorance in preference to knowledge. It would be better simply not to know certain things. Janet Street-Porter, doyenne of 'yoof' culture, often provokes strong reactions, but the recent disclosures about the decline of her fourth marriage must have tested all but the most squeamish.

It is reported that her toy-boy husband was bullied into marriage, paid a wage to perform menial tasks and offered the derisory sum of £3,500 to get out of her life. As is the way with marital breakdown, there are, of course, two sides. In the divorce affidavit, Miss Street-Porter claims that her husband attacked her with salad cream, squirting her all over from a squeezy bottle. He was evidently trying to get her attention at the time and says he was 'in a turmoil'. These factors scarcely mitigate the offence, but a sober judge might reasonably decide that Miss Street-Porter's alleged requirements for daily sex might have been more than enough provocation for a man to reach for his salad-cream squirter.

They say that love is blind, but one would require almost total sensory deprivation to be able to spend one's life with Miss Street-Porter. She is decidedly unbeautiful, in spirit as well as in appearance. Her voice, which has the noxious properties of paint stripper, cannot surely be God-given; it must be the work of some satanic force intent on harming human sensibilities.

The fact that her television programmes were a popular success is merely evidence of the perilous state of our young people. Youth culture feeds off brashness and banality, and celebrities who reflect those ephemeral qualities feed off youth culture in turn. As with the emperor's clothes, there is nothing actually *there*.

One of the mysteries of modern times is that someone can appear unattractive and foul-mouthed and still be venerated. I watched a fly-on-the-wall documentary of L!VE TV where Janet Street-Porter was managing director. Full of self-importance, she strutted around the studios, screaming at her colleagues and indulging in tantrums which would have upstaged any three-year-old. Yet everyone around her seemed cowed into submission.

The deference which she commands is a strange phenomenon; it seems to be completely unwarranted—exactly the opposite of what might be expected. I can only comprehend it in terms of what I call the Diana Vreeland syndrome. She was the legendary empress at *Vogue* and seemed to beguile everybody, yet she was by no means beautiful by normal standards. A well-known photographer, famous for his aesthetic acumen, once flew to New York hoping to do a shoot for *Vogue*. As he sat in a corner of her office he was unaccountably mesmerised by Vreeland. When she called him over, he heard himself say: 'I want to f*** you.' Truly, there is no explaining the workings of the human psyche.

23RD MAY 1997

Jodie Foster

The high price of betrayal

In Shakespeare's *Cymbeline*, the faithful Imogen, falsely accused of adultery, utters these momentous words: 'Though those that are betrayed/Do feel the treason sharply, yet the traitor/Stands in worse case of woe.' Since we live in times of increasing treachery, it is of some consolation that her words remain as true today as in 17th-century England. Natural justice invariably prevails.

The modern style of bad faith is the 'kiss-and-tell' genre, a tawdry trade which makes money for parasites from revelations about the private lives of their hosts. A particularly cheap variation on this theme is the book published this week by Buddy Foster, brother of the more famous Jodie. The startling 'revelations' amount to no more than the pitiful sentence: 'I always assumed Jodie was gay, or at least bisexual.'

Mr Foster admits that he has no actual evidence and that his comments are based entirely on assumption, rather than knowledge. But those trained in the business of making a fast buck know only too well that something can be made out of nothing, especially if the sexuality of the person concerned has been the subject of intense media speculation. Facts matter not at all; it is enough to hint and insinuate and hope that prurience will keep people reading.

One of the most disagreeable aspects of this opportunism is the appeal by author and publisher alike to some lofty code of ethics. Broadsheet newspaper editors invoke the public's 'right to know', and scoundrels like Major James Hewitt (an officer, but no gentleman) claim to have been motivated, not by greed and exploitation, but by a selfless urge to tell a touching love story of national importance. Who's kidding who?

Apart from dismissing her brother's book as cheap gossip, Jodie Foster has maintained a dignified silence. She is an exceptionally talented and intelligent woman, a brilliant actress and now an acclaimed film producer. Yet, like other high profile women, she is a victim of her own success. She has been prey to all manner of perverts, one of whom shot President Reagan in an attempt to gain her attention.

She has also been dogged by persistent rumours about her Sapphic leanings. As someone who believes that women are much more attractive than men, more interesting and generally superior, I can only applaud her good taste if that is the case. Yet we are still left with the question of betrayal, surely the most despicable example of human conduct.

I was once betrayed – not sexually, and not by a woman – although these factors did nothing to diminish the pain. Those who betray abuse friendship and trust, and they damage the lives of their victims. In time the harm can be assuaged, but it can never be totally eradicated. For 30 pieces of silver, Judas Iscariot betrayed Jesus to the priests of Jerusalem. Judas hanged himself from an elder tree. For betrayal, no redemption is possible.

30TH MAY 1997

Antonella Moccia

Drawing a Veil over Modern Life

People discover God in different ways but to leave the catwalk for the convent is no ordinary spiritual journey. Antonella Moccia, Italy's leading model, has stunned the world of fashion by giving up her glamorous life and taking vows of poverty, chastity and obedience. For the last 10 years she has modelled clothes for top Italian designers, but now she intends to devote herself to a life of prayer and contemplation.

We can only speculate on the reasons which lie behind such a momentous decision, but research suggests that some kind of inner crisis usually precedes entry into a religious community. Indeed the ascetic life is often regarded by psychologists as a coping mechanism after personal trauma. In Antonella's case, her vocation came after she watched her father die of cancer.

Most people have formed their impressions of nuns on the basis of Mother Teresa, or the singing mother superior in *The Sound of Music*, neither typical specimens. My own perception has a more vivid basis, since my earliest erotic frisson was occasioned by nuns. This is not the dreadful confession it might appear.

When I was a small boy growing up in the Holy Land I attended a convent school with my three sisters. Every morning my eldest sister took my hand and led me up the mountain track to the imposing abbey with the words *Dames de Nazareth* wrought on the huge gates. Inside we were exhorted to worship God, but I worshipped the nuns.

The convent was a place of deep mystery. The beauty and purity of the nuns, which contrasted with dark references to something called concupiscence, stimulated the boyish imagination. The atmosphere of the convent was profoundly sensual: the rich fragrance of beeswax and incense, the click of the rosary beads, the swish of starched black habits all contributed to the seductive process. None of this was registered consciously of course, but everything was imprinted.

I carried these impressions into adult life, but it is the mark of childhood that early memories never quite coincide with subsequent experience. I began to see nuns zooming along motorways in fast cars, or boarding planes as confidently as any businessman. Convents now have web sites on the internet, and it is no longer remarkable for nuns to carry mobile phones.

My state of confusion about the modern nun deepened when I interviewed Sister Wendy Beckett, art critic, author and television presenter. It struck an incongruous note to hear her speak of the lovely, fluffy pubic hair of Stanley Spencer's painting of his mistress, and when she said, 'Sex is, of course, something to cheer on', the embarrassment was all mine.

Sister Wendy is an elderly nun who reluctantly left her Carmelite monastery in Norfolk for the bright lights of television. Antonella Moccia has abandoned her celebrity status for the contemplative life, but I wonder if it is only a matter of time before the cloister and the catwalk are completely compatible.

6TH JUNE 1997

Jerry Hall

Why Jerry just keeps Rolling along

'In order to keep your man, you have to be a cook in the kitchen and a whore in the bedroom.' This was the wise counsel offered to the young Jerry Hall by her beloved Texan mother. To strive to combine the skills of Delia Smith with the talents of Fanny Hill is no doubt sound maternal advice, but if you are married to Mick Jagger, it seems more desperate measures are called for. To have another baby at the age of 41 is truly inspired.

Pandering to his every sexual whim failed to keep the Rolling Stone on the straight and narrow. Jerry once claimed that coitus took place each and every morning, a confession which made men up and down the land feel faint with envy. 'Even if you only have a few seconds,' she exhorted women, 'drop everything and give him sexual satisfaction. That way he won't want sex with anyone else.' The trouble is that Mick Jagger is a chronic Lothario.

Public infidelity is always deeply painful and humiliating for a woman. The misery of being a betrayed wife is a universal torment, but the range of options open to women is limited and unsatisfactory. At one extreme you can be like Madame Butterfly, wait faithfully for years and end up falling on your father's sword. At the other extreme, you can follow the example of David Bowie's long-suffering wife and join in the fun. She took to sleeping with her husband's lovers which led to some interesting threesomes. Somewhere in between you can choose the Stand By Your Man routine, much favoured by Tory wives.

The instinctive behaviour of many women is to blame themselves, but that way even greater unhappiness lies. Much better to be like Lady Graham-Moon who, with true panache, formed the Old Boys Club for wronged wives, although not before emptying her husband's wine cellar and slashing the crotches of his Savile Row suits.

Set against these role models, Jerry Hall has chosen what might be called the path of Positive Victimhood. This is proactive behaviour, skilfully championed by Princess Diana in That Interview, when she started off as a pathetic creature beyond pity and ended up as Queen of Hearts.

Jerry Hall has the perfect credentials to survive a difficult situation and turn the chaos of a nearly wrecked marriage into something creative and joyful. Graduating from a Bohemian lifestyle in Paris where she kept company with the black tigress Grace Jones, she became a famous model and wife of the ageing pop star. In 1993, she proposed the motion to the Oxford Union: 'This House believes that it is the duty of everyone to exploit their assets'. The motion was carried and last year, as Jerry approached her fortieth birthday, she displayed her own assets by letting her knickers drop enticingly inside the covers of *Vogue*. Now she is expecting her fourth baby. Undoubtedly she is a woman for all seasons.

17TH JUNE 1997

Pamela Armstrong

Doing What Comes Naturally

I am dismayed by the recent furore which followed the disclosure that Pamela Armstrong is still breastfeeding Alexander, her three-year-old son. I prefer to believe that Alexander is truly blessed.

Over the years mothers have been at the mercy of conflicting childcare experts who have been dogmatic about what children should be doing, or not doing, at every given stage of their young lives. Not so long ago, before feeding on demand became acceptable, babies were left to cry in their cots alone and distressed. Mothers were made to feel guilty if they picked up their babies outside the appointed hours of the regime.

One of the disturbing aspects of this advice is that it plainly controverted nature, in the sense that nothing could be more natural than a mother suckling her baby – not at times prescribed by a handbook, but according to the instincts of mother and child. Judging by the recent abuse heaped on Pamela Armstrong, however, it now appears that nature can be taken a step too far.

She has been accused of using her child to seek attention, of being aggressively middle-class and of stacking up a pile of psychological problems for her son in later life. None of these charges rings true. Pamela Armstrong – as I discovered when I talked to her – is perfectly sane and well-adjusted, an impressive woman with no axe to grind. She is to be admired for making the transition from career woman to traditional earth mother, a symbol of warmth and sensuality.

British society is in a state of lamentable confusion about women's breasts. The cultural rules which govern them reflect a rigid dichotomy: breasts can be either functional or decorative, but not both. The breasts which adorn the shelves of newsagents or grace the advertisements for fast cars and soft drinks are the same breasts which have to be discreetly hidden from public view when performing their natural function. The young, burgeoning breast is certainly a thing of exquisite beauty, but the fuller maternal breast also has its own magnificence, a source of intimacy and protection.

The most bizarre criticism of Pamela Armstrong is that she continues to breastfeed her child just for comfort. What can be wrong with comfort, I wonder? In this chaotic, benighted life there is too little comfort.

What our brave new world fears most is that sensuality might spill over into motherhood. It is not acceptable for maternal emotions to be compatible with a sense of physical fulfilment. But, in fact, many women derive great satisfaction from nursing their babies. A mother's bond with her child is often an intense physical experience, rather like falling in love.

In the part of the world in which I grew up, breastfeeding was unattended by dogma or neurosis. There were no fixed rules, only needs and desires. I was allowed to suckle for as long as I wanted, and this has undoubtedly contributed to a lifelong love and appreciation of the female breast.

20TH JUNE 1997

Marina Warner

So many men... so little time

The memorable words – 'So many men . . . so little time' – were those of Marina Warner when she spoke to me 10 years ago of the poignancy occasioned by the limitations of time and the power of sexual desire. During the interview I was mesmerised by her formidable intellect and the intensity of her beliefs, not to mention her soulful eyes and La Gioconda smile.

The news that the feminist and prominent academic has left her second husband and fallen in love again at the age of 51 has invited scorn from those who would judge her harshly. The fact that she is a former convent girl who once made a vow to model herself on the Virgin Mary will gladden the hearts of the gossips. My own view is different.

Marina Warner is without hypocrisy; indeed, she has always recognised the contradiction in her own character of believing one thing and practising another.

Most of us are decisively shaped by our earliest influences and during the rest of our lives we can only modify that which cannot be substantially altered. Marina's mother came from the warm, sensuous south of Italy; by contrast her very English father was a cultured Protestant who thought that Roman Catholicism was a proper religion 'for a girl'. At St Mary's Ascot, Marina was brought up in a stultifying creed which regarded sex as a terrible sin. 'Female desire was something the nuns wanted to pretend did not exist, or had successfully imagined did not exist.'

When she went to Oxford, female desire was established for her beyond doubt, and the existence of God was accordingly thrown into question. In 1964, when she spoke in favour of the motion 'That the miniskirt does not go far enough', the *Daily Telegraph* reported that her own skirt was made of silver foil and reached nine inches above her knee.

Thirty years on, Marina Warner became the first woman to deliver the prestigious Reith Lectures. Under the title *Managing Monsters*, she examined ancient myths which persist in contemporary culture. Significantly, the first lecture traced the idea of the independent woman – as in Greek myth – causing chaos and needing to be tamed. As she herself acknowledges, all myths contain a measure of truth.

When Marina parted company from the Church, she went on to write *Alone of All Her Sex*, which explores the cult of the Virgin Mary. Far from being a diatribe against the faith, it provides a fascinating study of traditional Catholic attitudes toward women and has a deeply spiritual dimension. Ultimately, however, the idea of the Madonna combining motherhood and chastity is fatally flawed. She is the figure in whom all contradictions are supposedly reconciled, but the double ideal she represents is unachievable by ordinary mortals.

That is Marina Warner's powerful thesis. And she herself is the perfect living example of her own deeply held conviction: that we are imperfect beings and our actions reflect what it means to be human and flawed.

27 JUNE 1997

Germaine Greer

For she's a jolly good Fellow

Consistency is famously the mark of small minds. Whatever else we think of Germaine Greer we must credit her in Emerson's terms with a very large mind indeed. Emerson, like Greer, was celebrated for his controversial views, and he exhorted people to speak out in words as hard as cannon balls without regard to whether each new view contradicted the last. 'With consistency a great soul has simply nothing to do,' he wrote.

Dr Greer's great soul has recently been busy causing a rumpus in the traditionally peaceful corridors of Newnham College, Cambridge, the all-female college where Greer is a lecturer and member of the governing body. According to the statutes of the college, all fellows must be women, but last year Dr Rachel Padman who started off life as a man was appointed a teaching Fellow. Dr Padman, a distinguished physicist, underwent a sex change operation in 1982. When she was invited to join the teaching staff she was anxious not to bring the college into disrepute; she therefore informed the principal of her medical history. The matter was duly considered and judged to be immaterial by the principal and other staff, who gave Dr Padman their wholehearted support.

But no one thought to consult Dr Greer. When the high priestess of feminism discovered last week that the college statutes had been contravened, she immediately went on the offensive with all guns blazing. 'Dr Padman's past was kept secret from us on the governing body. We were told by people outside the college making fun of Newnham and, frankly, we feel we have been made monkeys of.'

Somehow one might have expected Dr Greer to be on the other side, fighting prejudice and narrow-mindedness, telling those who made fun of a person's courage and pain to take a run and jump. Besides, such pedantic adherence to rules (especially rules devised in 1871) is surely out of character for a seeker after justice. Or is it?

The trouble with Germaine is that she can be characterised only in terms of the heavy artillery which she directs on to each new target. She is always passionate, angry and absolutely certain.

Twenty five years ago in *The Female Eunuch* she portrayed marriage and children as a legalised form of slavery for women. Years later in *Sex And Destiny* she romanticised the family ideal of southern Europe. She is a feminist icon who can rarely resist ingratiating herself with men. She once enjoyed a reputation for wild abandon, posing naked for a magazine called *Suck* with her ankles tucked behind her head. Later she championed celibacy, claiming that no sex was better than bad sex.

It has been part of her appeal and entertainment value that she has never known whether to keep her knickers up or take them down. But when they hang half-mast on the flag-pole of indignation, involving cruel public exposure of an innocent individual, Dr Greer looks somewhat ridiculous.

4TH JULY 1997

Kathleen Turner

The heat is on for Kathleen Turner

Kathleen turner is distinguished from the ordinary movie star by the sheer quality of her acting. There is therefore a certain irony in the fact that she is currently appearing in a one-woman show based on the life of Tallulah Bankhead, whose offstage personality was so scandalous as to prevent her being taken seriously as an actress.

Bankhead, who once described herself as being 'pure as driven slush', was a larger than life character whose stage appearances veered between the brilliant and the calamitous. Eventually the parties, alcohol and cocaine took their toll and her professional performances became unreliable. Noel Coward, in whose play *Fallen Angels* she took the lead, recalled an evening at Chez Paree: 'Tallulah screamed and roared and banged the table, and I wished the floor would open.'

Tallulah was outrageous for her time, revelling in her own exhibitionism. She was sexually ambiguous, claiming that sex was a private affair, simply the business of the three people involved. Like Mae West, she was mistress of the one-liner, often at her own expense. 'I've been called many things,' she once said, 'but never an intellectual.'

By contrast, Kathleen Turner is perhaps the nearest thing to an intellectual in the acting world. She is as impressive playing Shakespeare or Chekhov as she is in cinematic roles as different as *Romancing the Stone* or

The Accidental Tourist.

But it was in 1981 when she first ignited the screen as a voluptuous sex goddess in *Body Heat*. During the first 10 minutes of the film there is a succession of images of intolerable heat, with Kathleen Turner as the sizzling, sultry *femme fatale* at the very centre. She is sinister and mysterious, erotic and disturbing. 'You're not too smart,' she says to William Hurt, who plays a third-rate lawyer and local stud. 'I like that in a man.' On both sides of the Atlantic men mopped their fevered brows and longed to be less smart.

A few years later, in 1986, I met Kathleen Turner when she was playing in Pam Gem's *Camille* in Connecticut. She talked about her early life, how she was expected to make her own way, her attraction to Jewish men, her love for her husband and how she was aware that she frightened the hell out of men.

When it came to more personal matters, she told me she thought that most people were seriously disappointed in sex. 'For me, good sex, meaningful sex, is vital.' I had absolutely no difficulty in believing her.

Few stars have taken charge of their careers as intelligently as Miss Turner. She has avoided being typecast as a sex symbol, allowing her fine talent to be determined by each new role, rather than her star status. Tallulah Bankhead was ultimately a sad character, a victim of her own worst excesses. The same could never be said of Kathleen Turner; she plays the role with consummate conviction and touching humanity.

11TH JULY 1997

Sylvie Guillem

THE PRIMA BALLERINA WITH FIRE IN HER FEET

*L*ast friday, I attended the Royal Ballet at Covent Garden – the last occasion for the next two years, at least while the ambitious refurbishing programme is carried out. There was a valedictory air, but any impulse to melancholy was quickly dispelled by the sheer virtuosity of the performance given by Sylvie Guillem, surely the most exciting ballerina of her generation. She danced the lead in a work called *Steptext* set to the music of Bach's D minor Chaconne for solo violin.

Sylvie Guillem was born in Paris and first started dancing at the Paris Opera ballet school, where the regime is mercilessly hard. Only one or two of the annual 600 applicants make it into the *corps de ballet*. The discipline is such that the pupils normally become docile and submissive. Not so Sylvie Guillem; she emerged with personality intact and character in abundance.

When she was only 19, she danced the lead in *Swan Lake* at the Paris Opera House, just five days after reaching the level of *première danseuse*. As the curtain came down, the audience rose to their feet in a huge surge of emotion. There followed a soul-stirring moment, unprecedented in the history of ballet, when Rudolf Nureyev came on stage and announced that, as a result of the sheer brilliance of her performance, Sylvie Guillem was immediately to become an *étoile*, the highest rank in ballet.

More than a decade later, she is dancing better than ever. Sometimes technical expertise is lacking in emotion; perfection can often inhibit the expression of feeling. But this could never be said of Guillem, whose extraordinary flexibility combines with artistic subtlety in a most tender and moving way. Normally, ballerinas are creatures of such delicate physique and beauty that, like priceless pieces of porcelain, they are to be marvelled at, but not touched. They have a forbidding aura which prohibits sexuality.

Once again, Guillem is different. She is mysterious, erotic and exquisitely physical. She has sultry looks with a shock of red hair, and her beautiful, strong legs extend seemingly without limit. The choreographer Robert Helpmann once said that the fashion for nudity would never include dance because there are portions of the human anatomy which would keep swinging after the music had stopped. With Sylvie Guillem I do not believe it. Her body is so beautifully sculpted as to possess the still elegance of a statue.

When I was taught my catechism in a Catholic monastery, heaven and hell featured a great deal in our daily lessons. I grew up imagining heaven to be a rather dull place to which, in my adult life, I have never aspired. But if I could be sure that Sylvie Guillem is destined for heaven, I would be prepared to relinquish sin, at least for the last few years of my life. It is said that when the great Nureyev shouted at Sylvie, she screamed right back at him. There could yet be some fire in heaven.

18TH JULY 1997

Erica Jong

FLYING IN THE FACE OF CONVENTION

Fear of Flying was a novel which actually changed lives, before that particular phrase was rendered meaningless by over-use. It sold more than 15 million copies and became a landmark in feminist literature. Its author, Erica Jong, was bold enough to reveal to the world that women were also consumed by desire – still a relatively new idea in 1974 – and her name became synonymous overnight with the concept of the 'zipless f***'. Roughly translated, this meant a brief, anonymous encounter, or sex without guilt.

More than 20 years later, Erica Jong has published her latest novel, *Of Blessed Memory*, a story spanning the 20th century told through the lives of women. She has dedicated the book to her 18-year-old daughter Molly, who accompanied her to the UK on a publicity tour. Molly is Erica Jong's only child, the product of her mother's third marriage, which ended in an ugly divorce. Molly has the look of someone who has been forced to be wise beyond her years.

It is a popular belief that the children of famous parents carry a heavy load. If the relationship is on an intense one-to-one basis, and if your mother's reputation rests on the fact that she was a pioneer of the sexual revolution, then anything like a normal childhood is presumably impossible.

It has been difficult for many of the children of Erica Jong's generation, partly because people in the Sixties and early Seventies were experimenting in a way which had been impossible before the advent of the Pill. Erica Jong herself has admitted that there were no absolute certainties; a lot of her sexual philosophy, outspoken and sensational as it was, she made up as she went along. Behind all the shockingness, however, there was a genuine search for a kind of platonic ideal: 'The zipless f*** is absolutely pure. The man is not taking and the woman is not giving. And it is rarer than the unicorn.'

Fear of Flying was a genuine breakthrough novel, but before long it became the most politically incorrect book of modern times. Its author suffered from a new puritanism engendered largely by AIDS and the increasing prominence of rape as a political issue. The latter was seized upon by the feminists and Jong was attacked by the movement which she had once championed. Her personal life continued to be marked by difficult love affairs which usually ended badly.

None of this can have been easy for the young Molly, who does indeed have some of the credentials of a troubled life (drug-taking and the occasional death-wish). But there is much to be said for having Erica Jong as your mother. She is not like other feminists (she wears lipstick and high heels) and she is brilliantly irreverent and uninhibited. She also has a sense of humour, as this early poem demonstrates. 'If no man appeared who would love her/She would whip one up/Of gingerbread/With baking powder/To make him rise.'

25TH JULY 1997

Julie Christie

Turning her back on stardom

Sir Ralph Richardson once said that acting was the art of keeping a large group of people from coughing. This was a modest claim for a profession in which he reigned supreme, yet, like most aphorisms, it contains an element of truth. Most of us have endured evenings at the theatre where the coughs and splutters have reached the level of a bronchial ward in a hospital. It is difficult not to conclude that this has something to do with either the quality of the play or the standard of acting.

In the Minerva Theatre in Chichester, where Marguerite Duras' play *Suzanna Andler* is currently showing, there is scarcely so much as a clearing of the throat. This is almost entirely due to the mature acting skills of Julie Christie, who portrays the anguish of a woman married for 17 years and debating whether to abandon or continue the affair with her lover.

Duras' plays are famous for their introspection and analysis of *la condition humaine*. They do not lend themselves to great dramatic outpourings; everything is understated. The leading role in *Suzanna Andler* is immensely challenging, since it deals with a woman who is isolated by her inner conflict. But Julie Christie is equal to the challenge. She is completely in charge of her material and her stage presence is elegant and finely tuned.

There are very few film stars who can make the

transition to the theatre as impressively as Christie. This is perhaps because her cinematic career has been a significant test of her acting skills, unlike that of many contemporary female stars whose role is often decorative and heavily reliant on sex appeal. Though Christie has sex appeal in abundance, the theatre demands more profound qualities.

Julie Christie was elevated to stardom in the Sixties, a decade which she epitomised by defying convention. She was gloriously sensual in *Billy Liar* and, a few years later, she was the young and spirited Bathsheba in Schlesinger's *Far from the Madding Crowd*. In between, she showed her resistance to typecasting by starring in Truffaut's futuristic *Fahrenheit 451*.

In the Seventies, she was the luminous aristocrat in *The Go-Between*, displaying a range of complex emotions from love to cruelty. And who can forget the opening love scene with Donald Sutherland in *Don't Look Now*? It was so moving that many people thought it must have been real rather than simulated – thereby missing the point, since real lovemaking would not have convinced in the same way.

In 1978, she starred in *Heaven Can Wait*, the start of her commitment to political and social causes which have increasingly defined her cinematic roles. She has tackled the themes of nuclear disarmament and animal rights – hardly blockbuster subjects. By consciously casting off her star image, Julie Christie is nowadays more likely to be seen in small, uncommercial film theatres. But that is essentially where cinema is still art.

1ST AUGUST 1997

Tatyana Yeltsin

Boris Yeltsin's spin daughter

Boris Yeltsin does not regard himself as a superstitious man. But just before his wife was delivered of her second child, he placed an axe and a man's peaked cap under her pillow to ensure that she gave birth to a son. Things did not go according to plan, however, and another daughter – Tanya – was born. As if to compensate for her inferior status Tanya worked hard to make her father proud. She got top marks at school before going on to the prestigious Moscow State University. There she studied maths and cybernetics, specialising in the trajectories of spacecraft in orbit. Surely no son could have done more to please her father.

Daughterly devotion has recently been rewarded with an official appointment as her father's chief image-maker. This amounts to more than the cut of his suits and the sweep of his hair. At 37 she is the power behind the throne, capable of real political influence. Her appointment has provoked fierce opposition and allegations of constitutional violation.

Politics in Russia is traditionally a man's domain. It is a primitive world dominated by fear and suspicion. Even the closest presidential aides know that they can easily end up floating in the Moskva river. But daughters occupy a special place in their fathers' affections.

It was during the presidential elections a year ago

that Tanya was drafted in to help with what was tactfully described as her father's public relations problem. Yeltsin seemed to have been inspired by the example of Jacques Chirac whose daughter Claude took charge of his campaign. Tanya's task was more daunting; it consisted in marketing an ailing president who had succumbed to the temptations of absolute power. The electorate had become so cynical that something in the order of a miracle was required.

The miracle happened, and Yeltsin was elected to serve a second term. The spin daughter had transformed her father into someone recognisably human, less remote from the people. She had even persuaded him to shimmy on the dance floor. Tanya later took centre stage during Yeltsin's absence from office while he underwent critical heart surgery. She was the only person he trusted.

The relationship between Tanya and her father is preternaturally close – perhaps because of an early bonding experience. Once when his wife was ill, Boris had to take baby Tanya on a long train journey to be looked after by her grandmother. He had forgotten to bring milk, so after a while the baby began to scream and could not be comforted. He searched the train for a nursing mother, but to no avail. Eventually he opened his shirt and put the baby to his own milkless breast where she relaxed and fell asleep.

The lessons to be drawn from this are by no means clear-cut, but it is probably safe to say that a daughter who has been suckled by her father is destined for great things. The dawn of a new political dynasty is nigh.

8TH AUGUST 1997

Geri Halliwell

Adding some Spice with a bundle of fun

St Agnes, patron saint of virgins, lived at the beginning of the 4th century. She rejected all suitors and vowed that her body was consecrated to Christ, in the end preferring death to any violation of her virginity. She has been venerated by many nations.

Geri Halliwell, alias Ginger Spice, has recently opted for a chaste life, preferring celibacy to any revelations about her antics in the bedroom. She is also venerated by many nations.

Are these two young women, separated by centuries, linked in spirit by that most testing of virtues – celibacy? In the case of St Agnes, she was one of the earliest virgins and martyrs, but even before Christianity chastity was exalted. In ancient Rome the principal duty of the Vestal Virgins was to remain celibate. If they violated their purity, they were buried alive.

The great religious traditions of Hinduism, Buddhism and Christianity all have firmly established roles for celibate monks seeking their salvation. Some believe the highest spiritual experiences can occur only when individuals have given up worldly pleasures. Sexual abstinence is believed to place the individual in a state of grace.

It is difficult to see Ginger Spice as part of this long and noble tradition. Geri has renounced sex simply to prevent salacious details being revealed in kiss-and-tell stories in the press. The celibate usually bids farewell to the things of this world, not in order to avoid publicity, but the better to serve God.

I myself have never favoured the path of abstinence. Apart from the fact that the ascetic life has never appealed, I am suspicious of those who advocate self-denial and suffering as the way to God. I cannot believe that by sleeping on a bed of nails you have a better chance of entering the Kingdom of Heaven. I prefer the Woody Allen school of philosophy: in an ideal world love is the answer, but while you're waiting for the answer sex raises some pretty good questions.

Nor do I believe that the reasons for Ginger Spice's self-imposed celibacy are particularly valid, though they reflect the spirit of the age. 'Every time I have slept with a guy he ends up revealing to the world my most intimate secrets.' To deny herself pleasure because of possible press coverage is to allow the British culture of obsessive prurience – often masquerading as puritanism – to triumph. Far better to rise above it, or choose her men more carefully.

There is another alternative. In the 17th century and beyond people indulged in 'bundling', which meant going to bed with each other and cuddling, while remaining fully clothed. To bundle is an intransitive verb. That is to say, you cannot bundle anyone; you simply bundle by mutual agreement. Samuel Pepys was extremely highly sexed as we know from his diaries. He bundled in women's beds, but he rarely went further. According to Pepys, the practice was safe and highly pleasurable. Bundling might be the answer to Ginger Spice's problem.

15TH AUGUST 1997

Mel Thompson

LIGHTING THE WAY TO A MARKETING PLOY

We live in the Age of Science. Many phenomena, previously thought to be beyond human understanding, turn out to be explainable in terms of quantum physics, genetics or biology. Even those of us who resist scientific explanation and prefer to trust in God have had to come to terms with the Big Bang theory and the workings of DNA.

Yet, just as we were beginning to believe that science could explain everything, we learned last week that some poor woman's knickers caught fire at the Co-op in Wigan where she worked. Her name is Mel Thompson, a checkout assistant with no previous experience of the paranormal. After suffering a sensation of intense heat on her bottom, she immediately peeled off the sizzling undergarment, which by then had inflicted a three-inch burn.

Various theories have been advanced to account for Miss Thompson's misadventure, including a build-up of static electricity, or rare chemical reactions to a deodorant or washing powder. It has even been suggested that acid rain might have played a part. But, in each case, the probability ranges from low to virtually zero.

Spontaneous combustion – a particularly gruesome phenomenon which has affected a number of people in the past 100 years – invariably consumes the body, often reducing it to ashes while leaving the surroundings intact.

This theory could only be applied to Miss Thompson

in a very partial sense, and then only if we allow that her bottom somehow ignited the knickers, rather than the other way round.

If science cannot explain what happened, can religion shed any light? The Bible teaches us that the universe does not operate randomly, but is created and sustained in an ordered way by the Almighty. But, even allowing for the mysterious ways of God, it is difficult to understand what His purpose might have been with Miss Thompson in the Co-op.

Perhaps the answer lies in the extraordinary nature of fire. As one of the four basic elements, it has been ascribed magical properties since ancient times and considered a prime force in the cycle of purification and regeneration, with the added power of enlightenment. It was also a strong sexual symbol, based on the fact that fire was first obtained by up and down friction, an integral part of the sexual act. Just imagine the sales potential if a pair of pants could be invested with even some of these qualities.

Marks & Spencer, which retails the garment, is keen to distance itself from any suggestion that its knickers present a fire risk to women. But in so doing it seems to me it is losing a rare marketing opportunity.

For generations, the wearing of Marks & Spencer underwear has been synonymous with unadventurous living. A pair of St Michael knickers was always one of the great certainties in life. But the culture is changing; people are ready to live dangerously. If Miss Thompson agreed to promote this exciting new line, M&S could achieve record sales.

22ND AUGUST 1997

Demi Moore

Sense and cents ability

*D*emi Moore has recently been denounced by America's Southern Baptist Church for her latest role in the film *GI Jane*, to be released here next month, in which she plays a young navy lieutenant with a shaven head and profane tongue. To incur the wrath of Southern Baptists is not in itself difficult, although I find the evangelicals every bit as disturbing as anything Demi Moore might engage in. It is all a matter of perspective.

Demi Moore now seems to attract criticism from all quarters. She is currently one of the best-paid Hollywood actresses ($8 million for *GI Jane*) and perhaps this factor alone invites censure. Dancing on the bar in a 'bump and grind' routine with Madonna's brother in a Beverly Hills restaurant, or taking her clothes off for a talk show, have not helped her reputation as an exhibitionist. I take an altogether more benign view.

She has overcome great odds on the way to stardom. Her mother was an alcoholic and her father – who turned out to be her stepfather – committed suicide. She dropped out of school at 16 and dabbled in drugs.

She has also come a long way from her first major role in a film called *Parasite*, in which she had to scream a lot while trying to escape from a giant slug exhibiting roughly the same dramatic range as her own. But in *Ghost*, she displayed passion and sexuality with a rare conviction, and in *Striptease* – slammed by the critics –

I thought she was extremely credible.

Her biggest box-office success was the controversial *Indecent Proposal*, a modern Faust Story with Robert Redford playing the blue-eyed Mephistopheles offering her a $1 million wager.

In *The Scarlet Letter*, co-produced by none other than Dodi Fayed, she is seen lying in a bath, gazing at her own nakedness. In her husky voice, which has the power to make even the most banal off-stage statements sound profound, she tells her African servant: ''Tis only a bathtub, not a toy of Satan.'

Perhaps her best career move was in 1991, when she appeared on the cover of *Vanity Fair*, seven months pregnant and naked except for a string of pearls. I did not go along with her pretentious claim that it was meant to represent a fusion of fertility and female power, but I thought she had great chutzpah.

A few years earlier, she videotaped the birth of her first child and apparently likes showing it to friends. I adore Miss Moore's naked body, with or without the pearls, but I know in the squeamish depths of my being that I could not survive the birth video. Nor could I adopt her latest habit, which is to drink her own urine. But, since my medical dictionary tells me that 99 per cent of its mass is accounted for by water, sodium, potassium, calcium, magnesium and other organic compounds, perhaps her radiant eyes will soon have an added sparkle.

29TH AUGUST 1997

Arabella Pollen

Re-creation of a Queen of Fashion

According to Arabella Pollen in her first novel, *All About Men*, published today, the purpose of fashion people in the scheme of things is to save the world from drabness. As a fashion person herself until three years ago, famous for her tweeds, bright buttons and snappy suits, she injected plenty of colour into the world. Indeed, she was the epitome of Eighties success when she ran the eponymous Arabella Pollen fashion house, the haunt of royals and café society. International acclaim, however, could not save her from being a casualty of Nineties cutbacks.

My first encounter with Arabella was when she was 19. It was 1981 and I was involved in the production of JP Donleavy's play, *The Beastly Beatitudes of Balthazar B*. I used to stand in the foyer of the Duke of York's Theatre every evening, anxiously counting heads, eager for the play to succeed. One evening, I spotted a friend of mine who worked for *Vogue*. She wanted me to meet a young aspiring designer – Arabella Pollen.

Arabella was poised and energetic and her eyes were as blue and deep as the ocean. The combination of self-confidence and determination to succeed is very seductive – although I freely admit it was the eyes that clinched it. She could not sew, sketch or cut a pattern, yet I was happy to give her financial backing. I like risk and an element of adventure and, although our relationship was like a first love – with all its ups and downs and emotional excesses – I never regretted the decision.

Arabella had a good eye and a feel for fabric and colour, probably inherited from her grandparents who travelled the world and brought back acres of fabric – bolts of tweed from the Hebrides and embroidered cloths from the Far East. She designed her first collection and Diana, Princess of Wales, was one of her early clients, choosing a supremely elegant velvet-collared coat.

In 1984, Arabella wanted her brother Marcus to come into the business. I thought that three was a bit of a crowd and eventually we parted company. But we remained friends, and I was delighted when Arabella was backed by Courtaulds, the British textile giant. Three years ago, however, it withdrew its support and Arabella's company folded.

I admire people who have the courage to reinvent themselves, especially when they have suffered the slings and arrows of outrageous fortune. By switching from fashion to fiction, Arabella Pollen has done just that. Of course, writing a novel, particularly when it is as transparently autobiographical as *All About Men*, has become something of a cliché. The female protagonist Deli is recognisably Arabella and the warmth of Deli's relationship with her brother M is drawn straight from life. But it is a brisk read and the insights into the fashion industry are acute and incisive. More Jilly Cooper than Doris Lessing, but I feel sure the exercise has been cathartic.

5TH SEPTEMBER 1997

Charlotte Rampling

A Woman Born to Break Boundaries

*I*n 1973 when Charlotte Rampling starred in *The Night Porter*, she began to inhabit the dreams of a whole generation of men. I, for one, have never recovered from the sight of her straddling Dirk Bogarde, and the image remains in my mind like an old framed sepia photograph. In the film she plays a young girl who blossoms into a sophisticated woman, and her performance was so haunting as to move one leading critic to compare her to Garbo. Two years later in the 1975 remake of *Farewell My Lovely*, her seductiveness was supreme yet perfectly contained.

When I met her in the Eighties, the real Rampling was even more compelling than the screen version. She is exotic and English – a near contradiction in terms – and she underplays her sex symbol status with a rare intelligence, despite the allure of her emerald-green eyes, her velvety voice and the perfection of her bone structure.

Underneath the poise, however, Charlotte Rampling is haunted by demons. As the daughter of an army colonel, she had an itinerant childhood and suffered feelings of rejection by her mother who was besotted with her invalid sister. She reacted by exceeding the traditional boundaries of women's lives. During the Sixties, when everyone else was on CND marches or off in India doing ashrams, she went to live with gypsies in Afghanistan (a dangerous and violent experience) and later to a Tibetan monastery in Scotland.

By the time she was 22, she was in Hollywood and had earned herself the title of 'Europe's kinky sex film queen' by living in a *ménage à trois* with Brian Southcombe and a male model. When I interviewed her she told me she had loved both men but in order to spare her parents' feelings, she thought it best to marry one of them.

In 1976, she met Jean-Michel Jarre at the Cannes Film Festival after what she describes as a *coup de foudre*, and the following year they married. Jarre is a highly successful composer and musician with an international following. From the outside they seemed like a dream couple, combining art, beauty, glamour and intelligence in enviable proportions. It could have been an ideal partnership, but Charlotte Rampling was never likely to fulfil the Jane Austen view of marriage as a woman's principal act of self-definition. Rampling is far too unconventional ever to be defined by marriage. 'Jean-Michel and I are very *marginale*, as we say in French. We do things which are off the beaten track,' she told me.

Just as she has always chosen cinematic roles which explore the darker side of human nature, so she has delved deep into her own soul. She has suffered depression and come close to nervous breakdown more than once.

So far marriage has not brought her stability in the conventional sense; rather, it has been a continuation of a restlessness from which she has been unable to find refuge. *Plus ça change, plus c'est la même chose.*

12TH SEPTEMBER 1997

Rosa Monckton

The Power of a Mother's Love

In the emotional tidal wave since the death of Diana, Princess of Wales, millions of words have been written, soaking up the feelings of a stunned nation like blotting paper. One article which struck me as different from all the others was by Rosa Monckton. She had been a close friend of the Princess for 10 years and they had holidayed together in the Greek islands immediately before Diana's fatal trip with Dodi Fayed.

During that holiday, Rosa had the sense of being hunted along with the Princess and had promised her she would write about the cruel intrusion of the photographers. In the event, she wrote about a great deal more, simply and from the heart, and in a way which shed as much light on Rosa Monckton's own life as that of the Princess.

Rosa has forged a reputation for herself as a very successful businesswoman. She entered the jewellery world in 1981 and worked as head of public relations for Asprey during my own tenure there. Because she wanted to understand all aspects of the business, she studied gemmology and became skilled in the field. In 1986, she opened the London branch of the American jeweller Tiffany, which was where she met the Princess of Wales. As president of Tiffany, Rosa moves among the rich and cultured and enjoys a high social profile. Behind the scenes, however, away from the glamour and glitter, there is a powerful human story to be told.

Two years ago, Rosa gave birth to a Down's syndrome child. Rosa experienced deep emotions of grief and tenderness, the characteristic mix of mothers of handicapped children. Her husband Dominic Lawson, then editor of the *Spectator*, wrote about his newborn daughter with such love and candour that many people thought it the most moving article ever to have appeared in that journal.

Although Domenica's life expectancy is only half that of her elder sister's, it will be a rich life. After she was born, some cruelly insensitive people asked Rosa: 'Didn't you have the tests?' In stark contrast, Princess Diana offered herself as godmother and showed the intuitive compassion of which we have all become comprehensively aware. The year before, she helped Rosa bury Natalya, her daughter who died after being born prematurely. Both women knew heartache and understood each other's pain.

A few weeks' ago, Rosa Monckton came to lunch. She spoke about her daughters with such love and pride as would make angels weep. It takes courage to care for a handicapped child, and she does not underestimate the difficulties. Ironically, I envied her. I also felt a deep sense of humility.

In the space of a few sentences, she was more eloquent about the real implications of the sanctity of life than any number of bishops or banner-bearers. The sanctity of life is not some abstract principle; it is lived daily by people like Rosa Monckton who demonstrate the power of love and, by their example, increase the measure of humanity in the world.

19TH SEPTEMBER 1997

Ffion Jenkins

Ffion makes a Conservative decision

Mandy Rice Davies, notorious for her part in the Profumo Affair, once told me that power was the greatest aphrodisiac. According to her, men with power had 'a special glow – nothing to do with looks or intellect – just some strange chemistry which chops you at the knees'.

I wondered whether Miss Rice Davies' conviction might explain the enigma of Ffion Jenkins' betrothal to William Hague. Miss Jenkins is pretty, intelligent and talented – a woman of normally sound judgment and aesthetic sense. But even allowing that power and status are especially seductive, it is hard to believe that a little chopping at the knees should obliterate all other faculties. No, this is a mystery which I wish could be unravelled in order to promote greater understanding of the nature of love and attraction.

Ffion Jenkins is a high achiever in a family conspicuous for its successes. Mother is a magistrate, father is chief executive of the Arts Council of Wales, and sister is private secretary to the Prince of Wales. Ffion Jenkins is fluent in Welsh and gained four A-levels at school in Cardiff before going to Oxford. After graduating, she entered the accelerated promotion stream of the Civil Service and by the age of 27 she had soared to the private office of the Secretary of State for Wales.

Her relationship with William Hague blossomed when she taught him the Welsh National Anthem. After the general election, she was shrewd enough to resign from the Welsh Office. In so doing the future wife of the Conservative leader did not have to work with the new Labour administration. At 29, she has just been appointed director of the association of Business Sponsorship of the Arts, a high-profile, high-flying post.

There is no explaining all the elements which combine to make a successful marriage, but I cannot help feeling that William Hague has chosen well and Ffion Jenkins not so well. Love, of course, is a very personal business; it has no respect for laws of reason or objectivity. Indeed, like subjective truth, it is a commitment to believe in something which cannot be demonstrated or verified.

Women have traditionally been more sophisticated than men when it comes to choice of partner. Men have always set great store by physical appearance, but women are able to go beyond beauty and surface image, to look straight into the soul. On the evidence thus far, however, it is hard to believe that Mr Hague has much of a soul, particularly if he is wearing a baseball cap.

In a recent photo-opportunity, before the decisive vote on Scottish devolution, he was seen sitting on the edge of a boat on the banks of Loch Lomond, looking for all the world like a little boy who had lost his mum. At that moment my heart went out to the delectable Ffion Jenkins, for I had a terrible Flaubertian vision of the mortal boredom and emptiness which were the fate of Madame Bovary.

26TH SEPTEMBER 1997

Edwina Currie

A WOMAN WHO SPEAKS HER MIND

Jane Austen, in her earliest published work, describes a woman devoid of delicate feelings and refined sensibilities. 'As such,' she writes, 'we could scarcely dislike her – she was only an Object of Contempt.'

It is a subtle idea – that we might feel contempt without actually bothering to dislike. Perhaps this is a fitting response to Edwina Currie, who recently announced the end of her 25-year marriage during her promotional tour for her new novel, the aptly titled *She's Leaving Home*. Whether or not it was a cynical publicity stunt, there is no doubt that Mrs Currie has become an Object of Contempt. Pity, however, is surely more appropriate than hatred; Mrs Currie is not loved enough to be hated.

From the moment she entered Parliament in 1983, Edwina was champion of the photo opportunity. She regularly exercised her right to speak her mind, usually after she had assembled the nation's press.

She told her countrymen in the north that they were fat, smokers that they were disgusting, and exhorted the poor and elderly to knit woolly jumpers so that they could wrap up warm in winter. She is the archetypal WYSIWYG politician – What You See Is What You Get. The garishness of her clothes – checks and stripes, unappeased by floppy bows – is perfectly in keeping with her views and the way she expresses them;

Her first book, *A Parliamentary Affair*, is a near-perfect example of what is known in the trade as a 'dash for the cash'. It sold extremely well, not least because its publication in 1994 coincided with the most burning issue in politics – Tory sleaze.

It also won her second place in the *Literary Review*'s annual Bad Sex prize. The award is designed to draw attention to the crude, tasteless, often perfunctory use of redundant passages of sexual description in the modern novel, and to discourage it. Given the amount of frenetic coitus between its pages, the wonder is that the book was judged only runner-up. One particularly inelegant scene depicts a carton of strawberries, an aerosol of whipped cream and a Tory minister with improbable eating habits.

In the sequel, *A Woman's Place*, Mrs Currie favours tiramisu and chocolate sauce over the strawberries and cream. It is impossible not to associate the author with the novel's heroine, a flirtatious woman MP described as 'trim and delicious'. She stars in a number of bizarre copulatory episodes guaranteed to deaden a man's hormones.

She is also portrayed as blunt, opinionated, bossy and very pleased with herself. This suggests a degree of self-knowledge on the part of the author, but in life there is no obvious talent for self-improvement. Perhaps Mrs Currie cannot help herself. She grew up in a cold environment, starved of love.

Margaret Thatcher, aged nine, said after receiving a school prize: 'I wasn't lucky. I deserved it.'

I wonder if Edwina Currie, made in the same mould and with a similar level of self-belief, could say the same?

3RD OCTOBER 1997

Pamela Anderson

Playing the Mating Game

While I was in my house in the Dordogne recently I tuned in to CNN, a channel which displays the best of 24-hour news coverage. It offers an informative window on the world, but the 'fillers' – occasionally trivial and repeated items wedged between the main news reports – can lead a man to conclude that there are more interesting ways to spend the day.

One such story gave an account of the theft of an explicit sex video featuring *Baywatch* star Pamela Anderson and her husband Tommy Lee. Since the video was stolen some time ago, it hardly constitutes 'news', but apparently it has been copied and Miss Anderson is trying to stop its sale.

For someone who is completely and utterly a sex symbol – to the exclusion of everything else – it is surprising that she should mind so much. Only a few months ago, in front of nine million disbelieving viewers, she demonstrated her favourite coital positions with Ruby Wax in the back of a taxi.

Sex is Pamela Anderson's *raison d'être* and she makes a great deal of money out of it. *Baywatch* is seen in 140 countries by nearly two billion people, but it would be naive to suppose that this is on account of her acting ability.

Indeed, her début film, *Barb Wire*, in which she plays a leatherclad nightclub owner, showed that acting was too demanding an art form. Even the *Times*' critic, who was predisposed to admire a new talent, wrote that to call her performance wooden would be insulting to trees.

In truth, the size of Miss Anderson's audience is critically connected to the size of her silicone-augmented breasts. Of course, there are some people who believe that the possession of an enormous bosom is a talent in itself, but invariably they are men, and it is a delusion.

The fundamental question is: why should big boobs in themselves excite such staggering interest in men? For more than 50 years, our cinema screens have been packed with heaving bosoms: Jane Russell, Lana Turner, Diana Dors, Marilyn Monroe, Brigitte Bardot. But outside Hollywood it would be difficult to establish that breast size is related to sexual appetite. So why have we not learned from experience? Why are male fantasies so heavily visual, even when the objects of desire are artificial implants?

Michel Montaigne, the Dordogne's most famous literary son, wrote that there is no end to our researches. As if to honour his memory, my holiday reading included a work of fascinating research, *The Evolution of Desire*, by an American called David Buss.

It is a comprehensive study of human mating behaviour, suggesting that we are closer to our ancestral forebears than we might think. I scanned its pages for an explanation of the Pamela Anderson phenomenon. In chapter three I found it. It seems that millions of years of evolution show that men are attracted to women of high reproduction value. Women who are well-endowed signify health and fertility. Our liking for big breasts is therefore inbuilt. We can do nothing against it.

10TH OCTOBER 1997

… Nicola Horlick

What You Lose When You Have It All

An early experience of childhood terror was seeing one of those Victorian dolls, round-faced with painted lips, smooth and waxy complexion, and a neat fringe. There is something of the Victorian doll about Nicola Horlick, author of *Can You Have It All?*, the story of her life published this week. Mrs Horlick's round and painted features have disturbing mask-like qualities, a simulation of the real thing.

Her autobiography is equally intimidating. Successes and achievements are listed in passionless prose without a trace of self-doubt, and they make for exhausting reading. Such a book should come with a health warning. I kept wanting to curl up on the sofa with a hot-water bottle and listen to soothing music – something Mrs. Horlick would never do. She is too busy with unit trusts, planning the next baby, cooking, shopping, entertaining, buying quality homes in London, moving billions of pounds.

In January Mrs Horlick battled against Morgan Grenfell for unfair dismissal, and in the process she achieved star status. Most newspapers ran David and Goliath type stories, with Mrs Horlick emerging as a heroine refusing to be crushed by the giant Philistine bankers. With the press and cameras in tow, she flew to Frankfurt to the offices of the parent company. There she handbagged a hapless security guard, threatening to call the police if he laid a finger on her. The newspapers loved it, and next day there were dramatic headlines such as 'Superwoman Goes to War'.

Back home she stage-managed her PR with the same steely efficiency required for her success as a fund manager. Boadicea became Earth Mother. She wheeled a pushchair, cradled a baby to her breast, posed with four of her five children in Holland Park and cast herself in the role of victim. She told reporters she was 'unemployed with a mortgage to pay' – a remark which showed cruel insensitivity to those who struggle to make ends meet. This is the unacceptable face of capitalism.

She also talked of male jealousy and claimed that no man in her position would have been so shabbily treated. Would any man have paraded his small children so shamelessly, I wonder?

The author of *Can You Have It All?* is not a role model for women. Hardly anyone could be like Nicola Horlick – a great mercy in my view. It takes a very special kind of woman who can make a successful presentation worth £750 million to Morgan Grenfell when her eldest child's life is threatened by leukaemia. She does not suffer from guilt. She is completely driven.

If Mrs Horlick were a character in a novel we would relish the details of her self-righteous perfection in the certain knowledge that her downfall was being saved for the last chapter. In the final reckoning she would be punished by the author, and justice would be done. Mrs Horlick, however, is not a fictional creation; she is absolutely for real. But there are few human frailties to endear her to us. Like baked Alaska, she's cold in the middle.

17TH OCTOBER 1997

Cristina Odone

An Energetic and Enterprising Woman

*J*greatly enjoyed Monday evening when I was invited to the Ivy for cocktails. The occasion marked the publication of Cristina Odone's second novel, *A Perfect Wife*, which promises to be a polished successor to *The Shrine*.

Her first novel was full of passion, dealing intelligently with sex and religion, the sacred and the profane – a combination which has proved irresistible to many writers. Cristina Odone is well placed to write with conviction and authority on this theme. As a Roman Catholic with a strict convent education behind her, she struggles to live a disciplined life. But she is the first to admit that lust can exert a fearsome power, even on the devout. (The men who fall at her feet find it quite powerful too.)

From her Swedish mother and Italian father she has inherited that tantalising mix of northern poise and Mediterranean ardour. It is the southern heat which prevails, however. She exudes a deep sensuality and flirtatiousness, and has always said that she would be a very bad girl were it not for her faith. Just the sort of statement which is guaranteed to feed a man's fantasies. Her vocabulary is enchantingly biblical – sin, temptation, evil, grace are all regulars.

I have always felt a natural sympathy with Cristina Odone. We are both Catholics, highly volatile, both conscious of the challenge of the faith. I also attended a convent where one learnt the seductive power of religion. Indeed there's nothing quite like being taught by nuns to put the hormones into overdrive. There is such emphasis on the sinfulness of everyone, the carnality of the world.

Until she resigned last year, Cristina edited the *Catholic Herald*, a previously moribund organ which she transformed into a smart read. During her reign she fanned the flames of fundamentalist fury against trendy liberals in the Catholic church.

Three years ago we had a minor tiff. For St Valentine's Day, the *Catholic Herald* ran a spoof lonely hearts column in which conspicuous Catholics such as Auberon Waugh and Lord Longford were invited 'to pen their hearts' desire'. I entered into the spirit by concocting what I thought was a suitable entry. It began: 'Mature man of parts, with distinctive catholic taste for the unusual, seeks enduring relationship with energetic and enterprising woman.'

At the same time, in a fit of mischief, I sent a more explicit version for Cristina's eyes only. Next day, the *Evening Standard* ran a naughty item under the headline: Naim and his Catholic Tastes in Love. It suggested that my contribution had needed rigorous censoring in order to make it suitable for the *Catholic Herald*. When I discovered that Cristina herself was responsible for the story, I was furious. But not for long.

Some might say Cristina gives Catholicism a bad name. Not me; I think she is its very lifeblood. At 37, she is still searching for the man of her dreams. The lucky devil who marries her will gain a wonderful wife and excellent breeding potential.

24TH OCTOBER 1997

Jacqueline du Pré

A LIFE ENHANCED BY PASSION AND GENIUS

Ten years ago, the brilliant cellist Jacqueline du Pré died at the age of 42. At the end, she was completely paralysed by multiple sclerosis, unable to see or even talk.

In 1961, at the age of 16, she had made her début at London's Wigmore Hall and completely captivated her audience. The professor of cello at the Guildhall School of Music described her playing as 'the perfect marriage between real passion and innocent reverence . . . a spiritual, not just a physical thing'. The critics hailed her as a genius.

Throughout history, artistic genius has been a double-edged sword. It has been allied with madness and all manner of sexual profligacy, so perhaps it was only a matter of time before Jacqueline du Pré's brilliance was rewritten in these terms.

To mark the tenth anniversary of her death, Hilary and Piers du Pré, sister and brother of Jacqueline, have published what they describe as an intimate memoir, *A Genius in the Family*. Both Hilary and Piers believe the truth about their sister's life has been obscured by her public image.

Their account seeks to expose the 'fragile spirit' which lay behind Jacqueline's talent and beauty. Roughly translated, this means they are both fed up with their sister's saintliness, and resentful that it was Jacqueline who was so richly endowed. Hilary in particular, a talented flautist, clearly longed to be the musician her sister was.

At first the siblings paint a cosy family picture with picnics and jolly hols and pet names. Some passages read like Enid Blyton. Then come the shocks. Jacqueline had a vicious temper; she was demanding, unstable and sexually voracious.

A few years after her marriage to Daniel Barenboim, she suffered a serious nervous breakdown. For more than a year, she lived with Hilary and had frequent sex with Hilary's husband, Kiffer Finzi. Hilary knew and colluded.

Jacqueline's sexual appetite is presented as an aspect of her mental instability and the illness which was eventually to take her life. Hilary is stoical about her sister's excesses – her own husband was 'just trying to help' – and the betrayal is recounted in a spirit of Christian martyrdom.

The time has come to remove our prejudices about women and sex. For centuries, female passion has been linked with evil or instability. Witches were invariably thought to be sexually rampant and 19th century doctors thought mental disorders originated in the womb. These attitudes have continued, in subtler form, to the present day.

I have long supposed that God – who made us the gift of sex – takes a more enlightened view than Man. Sexual morality is shaped not by God, but by bourgeois attitudes and the prevailing hypocrisy. Christ preached a gospel of love and sharing.

Jacqueline du Pré was gifted and dynamic and sensual. Many people remarked on the sexual energy which came through in her art. If she was passionate in life, it is hardly surprising. But her memory is not now besmirched; rather it is enhanced.

1ST NOVEMBER 197

Melissa Butler

A VERY TEASING QUESTION

The handbook of the Oxford University Careers Service urges students to consider moving away from the most traditional careers. Instead of sticking to the time-honoured professions, it suggests flexibility is the only way to retain the advantage an Oxford degree can offer.

Melissa Butler, a second-year Philosophy, Politics and Economics student, has taken flexibility to interesting lengths. By day, she attends lectures at one of Oxford's oldest colleges; by night, she gyrates for the punters at the Sunset Strip in London's Soho. She recently appeared in a TV documentary, *The Grafters*, and seems to have taken the media interest in her stride.

'Strippers aren't supposed to be intelligent,' she says, 'and Oxford students aren't supposed to become strippers – at least not in the popular imagination.'

Not in the scholastic imagination either, it seems, for Miss Butler has ruffled the cloisters with a whiff of scandal. She knows that even to name her college would threaten her academic career. I believe the college should take a more relaxed view.

The university prospectus claims that the study of PPE will 'help a student to understand the social and human world, and to develop skills useful for a whole range of future careers and activities'. In these terms, Miss Butler could be regarded as a model PPE student.

Besides, strip-tease has always given rise to fears of

wanton vice and depravity. In our own century, the Public Morality Council campaigned vigorously for prohibition and prosecution. Council observers toured strip-clubs and warned darkly that such places were debauching the public (they themselves were evidently immune from harm). In their 1960 Annual Report on Public Morals, they expressed concern about a strip-boom in London. 'We greatly fear what tolerance of this kind of thing will lead to.' It is vital that our oldest university, a place of wisdom and enlightenment, should rise above the narrow minds of the moral police.

The feminist view of stripping was not so much concerned with immorality or indecency; rather, the stripper was a victim of male exploitation, degraded by indulging men's fantasies. But now we live in the age of post-feminism.

This means, among other things, that the stripper is someone who has taken charge of her own body. Far from being degraded by removing her clothes, she is empowered by it. Miss Butler describes herself as a 'delectable sex-goddess', but that's OK, because she is in control.

Alas, nothing is ever quite as it seems. Behind the poise lies a sad story which includes anorexia, binge-eating, membership of Mensa from the age of 12, high family expectations, low self-esteem. Stripping seems to be another stage in a deeply troubled personality. 'All the satisfaction I have known in my short life has come from taking my clothes off in front of men,' says Melissa. Now that *is* cause for concern.

7TH NOVEMBER 1997

Amy Homes

A SERVING OF PRETENTIOUS NONSENSE

Not so long ago, respectable publishers of literary works were tried under the Obscene Publications Act, something which made Britain the laughing stock of the Western world. In 1959, Penguin Books was in the dock over its proposal to publish *Lady Chatterley's Lover*. The absurdity of the trial was palpable when Mr Griffith-Jones, counsel for the prosecution, asked the jury if Lawrence's novel was one they would wish their wives or their servants to read. The jury, 12 good men and true, delivered a unanimous verdict of not guilty.

Banning books is something we no longer do. Artistic freedom is sacrosanct, and that is as it should be. Besides, we are inured to violence, we know the world is a terrible, benighted place and, though that may sadden us, it does not shock in the way it might once have done.

So what are we to make of the call by the NSPCC to ban *The End of Alice*, a book which purports to be the correspondence between a convicted paedophile and a 19-year-old woman who has seduced a young boy? The chief executive of the NSPCC has described it as the most vile and perverted novel he has ever read. He also wonders 'what kind of human being could write such stuff'. The answer is Amy Homes, an American woman, aged 35, a creative writing teacher at Columbia University. She guards her own privacy and is chillingly detached.

The End of Alice is by no means an everyday tale of perversion and paedophilia. This is as nasty and unpleasant a book as anyone is ever likely to read. It makes *The Silence of the Lambs* seem like a Sunday School picnic. Children, we learn, are complicit in their abuse; indeed, little Alice asks for it. The 12-year-old provokes her own death, is stabbed 64 times and beheaded. Before that she has been penetrated with knives and bottles and firearms. And that is by no means the worst of it. The 'voice' throughout is that of the paedophile; none of his acts of unspeakable vileness is challenged. Miss Homes says she wants us to understand the mind of the paedophile.

She is also very pleased with herself. 'As a writer you get a really great feeling. All this furore tells me I've got it right.' She denies that her novel condones sexual abuse, or feeds the fantasies of the paedophile. (Professionals who treat sex offenders disagree.)

'If the book gives the reader nightmares,' she claims, 'it means the reader was made to think on multiple levels. I'm all for thinking.' This is pretentious nonsense. Having nightmares is hardly the same as thinking. Miss Homes has detailed the 'how' in sickening detail; she has not explored the 'why'. There's not much to be learned from the cesspit, except that it stinks.

Does art have a duty to be moral? I am not sure of the answer to that. What I do know is this: Amy Homes' heartless novel is not moral. Nor is it art.

14TH NOVEMBER 1997

Santa Palmer-Tomkinson

An unfashionable act of love

Of the 600 guests at recent celebrations for the 25th anniversary of Quartet Books, there was one young woman whose beauty shone out from the smoke-filled rooms of Dartmouth House in London's Mayfair. This beacon of loveliness was the radiant Santa Palmer-Tomkinson, sister of the more famous Tara.

Santa was accompanied by her fiancé, the journalist Simon Sebag-Montefiore, whom she plans to marry in January 1999. The reason for the somewhat distant wedding date is that Santa is undergoing instruction in the Jewish faith and her conversion will take a year to complete.

Simon Sebag-Montefiore comes from a distinguished Anglo-Jewish family, aristocratic in origin and strong on tradition. Although liberal Judaism plays down observance of the stricter rituals, 'marrying out' is not encouraged. Indeed, marriage to a Gentile is scarcely considered a proper marriage.

Some will see Santa's conversion to Judaism as merely a means of tying the knot. Elizabeth Taylor adopted the Jewish faith to marry Mike Todd, and had five more husbands after that. But a lifelong commitment is not usually undertaken lightly; and Santa is very committed.

There are many different reasons for holding a particular belief, but by far the most common is the fact of being born into a certain religious tradition and imbibing the faith at an early, uncritical age. As a cradle Catholic, born and brought up in what was then Palestine, I am conscious that my own faith was no more than an accident of birth. Although my part of the world has been torn apart by religious strife, I have not yet been put off religion. It seems natural to cling to the faith in which I was reared, which makes me in awe of converts, none more so that Santa Palmer-Tomkinson. (The name Santa has a wonderfully saintly ring to it, although it seems her landowner father named her after a successful crop.)

A 'conversion experience' is generally understood to be a moment of blinding light and sudden revelation, as happened to Paul on the road to Damascus. Something similar happened to Hugh Sebag-Montefiore, a relative of Simon's, who at the age of 17 saw a vision of Christ and went on to become a Roman Catholic priest and one of that church's most influential figures. By one of those strange ironies, I published his biography. Montefiore suffered anguish at being cast out by the Jewish community, although his parents never withdrew their love. In the same spirit of enlightenment the Palmer-Tomkinsons are supporting their daughter.

At the end of the 20th century, it is not fashionable to be religious, far less to go through with conversion. We live in an increasingly secular age; Nietzsche's slogan 'God is dead' has never been more obvious. It is therefore an act of great moral courage when someone undertakes the difficult business of a new religion. As far as I know Santa has seen no dazzling lights, but to act out of love is very moving indeed.

21st November 1997

Myra Hindley

Why We Can't Let the Mob Rule

In 1966, Myra Hindley, along with her lover Ian Brady, was convicted at Chester Assizes of a series of murders so vile and repugnant that their power to shock has remained constant for more than three decades.

The victims were tortured before they were killed and their anguished cries were tape-recorded. When the voice of 10-year-old Lesley Ann Downey was played to the jury, it was uniquely horrifying. John Stalker, who went on to become deputy chief constable of Greater Manchester, said of the tape: 'Nothing in criminal behaviour, before or since, has penetrated my heart with quite the same paralysing intensity.'

In the intervening years, Myra Hindley is said to have become increasingly obsessed with the idea of her eventual freedom, and has made strenuous efforts towards that end. She has by turns pleaded her innocence, reaffirmed her guilt, been silent for long periods, and been openly contemptuous of public opinion. She has even returned to Roman Catholicism, her childhood religion. According to Lord Longford, who has long championed her cause, she is a sincere Christian and has shown herself capable of remorse.

Does it matter what Lord Longford believes? Not much, in my opinion. I am always suspicious of a man who presumes to know the extent of a person's faith and penitence, and his campaign on Hindley's behalf has been too high-handed and too pious.

What *does* matter is that the sentence was 30 years, and she has now served her time. We cannot keep extending her sentence. Hindley challenges every gut impulse we possess, but our system of justice must not bend to primitive emotions. Public revulsion is understandable, but it should not be the guiding principle in legal procedures.

Hindley believes she is a totem of 'tabloid moralism'; she complains of a 'lynch-mob rationale' being put before human rights. She is in no position to talk about human rights, but she is right about the lynch mob. There is no shortage of would-be executioners.

After 30 years, emotions are still running high. Unlike Brady, who is mad and has no expectation of being released, Hindley has become firmly established in the popular imagination as the very personification of evil. On Monday's *Panorama*, Kelvin MacKenzie, former editor of the *Sun*, shamelessly whipped up our basest instincts. He offered no reasoned argument, only venom. It was an unedifying spectacle.

Jack Straw, the Home Secretary, has also bowed to brute unreason. By deciding to keep Hindley incarcerated for the rest of her life he has shown moral weakness and cowardice. His judgment pre-empted the judicial review, and was almost certainly unlawful.

I am no defender of Hindley, but it cannot be right to manipulate the law, to treat someone as demonic, or allow summary justice to take place in the gutter press. And if we do not grant the possibility of redemption, then the whole of Christianity is nullified.

28TH NOVEMBER 1997

Countess Spencer

Following the Law of the Jungle

There is an Indian tribe called the Kuikuru who live in the jungles of Brazil. Adultery is a basic part of their way of life and it is accepted as the norm. Although a certain amount of discretion is judged appropriate, the popular assumption is that married couples will take lovers, up to 12 during the marriage.

If only Lord Spencer and his wife had moved to the Brazilian jungle instead of South Africa, then their divorce proceedings might not have become so acrimonious. The 12 women with whom Lord Spencer is alleged to have committed adultery would have fallen within acceptable limits.

As it is, the Anglo-Saxon world is not as relaxed about these things, even though we know from our history books that the aristocracy have traditionally married for dynastic security, and sought sexual pleasure elsewhere.

I first met Earl Spencer's wife – Victoria Lockwood as she was then – in 1987. She was a successful model at the time and living in New York above a Mexican restaurant in First Avenue. She shared an apartment with a young woman from my publishing house in Park Avenue South, and the three of us often went out together. Victoria was at the height of her career, but she was already showing signs of the problems which were to blight her married life.

When her engagement was announced in July 1989, it

was greeted with consternation in aristocratic circles. Charles Althorp could have had his pick of blue-blooded young things, yet here he was marrying a commoner, part of the *demi-monde* and trendy set. When Raine Spencer, Charles's stepmother, was asked about the union, she curled her genteel lip and intoned: 'Victoria is a beautiful girl with wonderful bone structure.'

Three months later, Victoria arrived at the church in a horse-drawn coach bearing the Spencer family crest. By the time she walked down the aisle, she had assumed honorary status as an aristocrat.

By April 1995, the marriage was effectively over. Victoria was in a private clinic in Surrey receiving treatment for eating disorders and addiction problems. She had already borne four children – the last, Louis, the son and heir. The separation was described as 'entirely amicable', a phrase which often sounds the death knell of any kind of harmonious divorce.

If the inglorious warfare between the Spencers demonstrated anything, it is that men of noble birth and the lovely women they marry sometimes lead wretched and absurd private lives.

In the passionate funeral oration to his sister, Earl Spencer showed the world that he adored Diana, and was sensitive to her pain. Victoria's difficulties, remarkably similar in kind, deserve the same degree of compassion. They should not count against her when it comes to financial arrangements. Men of noble birth should behave nobly, not meanly. Victoria is the mother of Earl Spencer's children, and by virtue of that fact alone, she merits the most generous settlement possible.

5TH DECEMBER 1997

Gillian Wearing

MODERN ART NOT WEARING WELL

More than 80 years ago, Marcel Duchamp, the French-born American painter, placed a urinal in a gallery and called it art. By all accounts he seems to have shocked his generation and, while that may have been a good thing, there is no evidence that Duchamp's *pissoir* has endured as anything other than an eccentric hoax.

In our own time, the urinal has many weird and wonderful successors. Recent artistic offerings have included the severed halves of cow and calf preserved in formaldehyde, frozen urine, dead shark, heaps of car tyres, pickled sheep, elephant dung and a tent sewn with the names of the artist's lovers.

The focus of our contemporary art scene has been the annual Turner Prize, worth £20,000 and described as 'Britain's most prestigious and serious visual arts award'. Last week it was won by Gillian Wearing, who specialises in something called 'confessional video'. One of her main exhibits was called *60 Minutes Silence* which shows a squad of police officers in what appears to be a group photograph. Only the twitching and blinking reveal that it a video, not a photograph.

Anyone who dares to ask whether this constitutes art is dismissed as philistine. And if you consider it merely dull, you are told that one of the duties of modern art is to explore the nether regions of tedium. For in the world of the Turner Prize nothing is quite as it seems. Anything which appears meaningless is actually full of significance, the banal is somehow exhilarating, the boring is brilliant and the pretentious is, in fact, a study of the reality of modern existence.

The chairman of the Turner Prize jury says that Gillian Wearing is an artist dealing with strong emotional issues. What are these emotional issues? The brochure at the Tate Gallery, where Wearing's work is on show, claims that 'she yields insights into the complexities of everyday life at the end of the 20th century'. But, in truth, it is impossible to know what these insights might be, or how we might learn from them.

In Hans Christian Andersen's famous story, the emperor's new clothes were supposedly invisible to unworthy people and it took a young, innocent boy to point out that the emperor was, in fact, naked. It is time to recapture the innocence of that young boy.

Modern art has been corrupted by its own hype and has less to do with creative talent and more to do with a terrible loss of faith. Ideas are not enough; it is the quality of their expression that counts. There is nothing wrong with running a camera for an hour, but it does not necessarily count as art.

The fidgeting police officers demonstrate nothing more profound than the difficulty of keeping still for an hour. Gillian Wearing doesn't engage me; she doesn't make me think. She makes me long for what we used to call art.

13TH DECEMBER

Helen Mirren

CLEVER BONKS

Some time ago I read a novel by Alice Munro which expressed the view that sex was something which no woman – at least no *intelligent* woman – would ever submit to unless she absolutely had to. Helen Mirren, star of the recent TV drama, *The Painted Lady*, is surely the living proof against such an idea. It is difficult to imagine anyone less bimbo-like; but she is an utterly convincing and accomplished bonker.

In her latest role, she plays an ex-blues singer with a chequered past, washed up on the shores of recovery after a dissolute life of drugs and bitter-sweet memories. She has a gold stud in her nose and a young chap in her bed. Three more by the end of the second episode.

Helen Mirren is a fine actor, whether on stage or screen. She is ambitious, but not in a crude way and, since her loveliness is unorthodox, it is all the more interesting. She started off at the age of 20 in the Royal Shakespeare Company and was thereafter credited with putting sex into Shakespeare.

In the early Seventies, perhaps because of a readiness to remove her clothes, she appeared in some truly dreadful films such as *Caligula* and Ken Russell's *The Savage Messiah*. But in 1984 she won Best Actress Award in the 1984 Cannes Film Festival for her part in *Cal*, and more recently she was nominated for an Oscar for *The Madness of King George*. As DCI Tennison in

Prime Suspect, she is gritty and professional, but also vulnerable, her appetites not quite held in check by the constraints of her job.

In 1994, I saw her as Natalya in *A Month In The Country*, Turgenev's study of unthinkable love. She brought such sensitivity to the role: having fallen for her son's tutor, she conveys the yearning, the being sick with love, the idea that it can strike unbidden at any time and make you appear foolish. One knew, just by her stage presence, that she had experienced that kind of demented passion.

Helen Mirren, in life as in art, is famously passionate. She once admitted to setting her alarm early every morning so as to have time to make love to her partner, the film director Taylor Hackford. She has a love-hate relationship with Los Angeles where classical acting is virtually unknown and older women are either ignored or surgically altered. She has exiled herself for love, but she returns from time to time to remind us that her eroticism and quiet maturity are a devastating combination.

It is always difficult to decide whether Helen Mirren brings intelligence to sex, or whether she manages to gild the intellect with an irresistible sensuality. Whichever it is, the process is rewarding and absolutely compelling for her audience. At 51, she can teach young starlets a thing or two, not least that youth and surface beauty are among the less interesting qualities when it comes to consummate acting.

20TH DECEMBER

Diana Mosley

Lies and Punishment

A review in this newspaper of a new biography of Mussolini reminds us that since the downfall of *Il Duce*, Italy has had 54 different governments, not to mention countless murders of politicians and other public figures. The fact that Italy is, of course, no longer a fascist state, but a democratic republic is a piercing irony. The review also points out that Mussolini fought for the Allies during the Great War and that he did a great deal for his country that was positive, such as building roads and suppressing the Mafia.

The reviewer was none other than Diana Mosley, something which will have made many readers wary of its contents. For Diana Mosley is the widow of Sir Oswald, leader of the British Union of Fascists. That alone is enough to make anything she writes suspect – at least to those whose minds are closed.

In 1991, I interviewed Diana Mosley at her country house outside Paris where she has lived for the past 50 years. She was devoted to Oswald and considered him to be visionary (the collapse of socialism in Europe being one example). Although she deplores the Nazi atrocities, she believes the biggest crime was the war itself, and that the horrors were not confined to one side.

Her sister Unity, who adored Hitler, shot herself when war was declared. Diana loved her sister and refuses to condemn the man she knew, for he kept his promises to the people and in their despair he gave them hope.

She has stuck to her views despite constant vilification, believing it 'monstrously unfair to deny something when I felt it very strongly at the time'. She has never followed the fashion; as one of the redoubtable Mitford girls, she was her own person right from the start. She has composure and charm in equal measure and even in her eighties seems to have been sculpted by the gods. Her perfect manners match her noble birth, and in that sense she is a true aristocrat, perhaps the last of her breed.

There is no arrogance, only a quiet humility. When she was interned in Holloway prison during the war, Churchill told the authorities she was to be allowed a bath every day. She refused, insisting that the one foul bathroom was to be shared equally among her 60 fellow prisoners who had become her friends.

In her youth, Diana's beauty was legendary. When I asked if this had made a difference to her life, she answered no, it had not. A few years later, in 1995, I received a letter from her saying that her answer had not been strictly honest and that it had indeed made a great impact on her life to have been *considered* beautiful. 'I am now punished for my lie,' she wrote, referring to the cancer in her nose which had required drastic surgery.

If lies are punished, then so sometimes is truth. Diana Mosley, who has told the truth as she remembers it, has been doubly and unfairly punished.

27TH DECEMBER